REV. FATHER EPHRAIM TAUCK

ANONYMOUS DIALOGUES

DISPELLING MYTHS CONCERNING THE RENOWNED PRAYER OF THE HEART

MOUNT HARVARD PUBLISHING

Icons and Artwork courtesy of Orthodox Arts Journal. Orthodox Illustration Project (orthodoxartsjournal.org).

Cover Art Work by the Anonymous Hesychast author of these works.

Back Cover quotes:

- St. Ignatius Brianchaninov *"On the Prayer of Jesus,"* (St. John of Kronstadt Press, 1995, page 17).
- St. Theophan the Recluse *"The Art of Prayer"* (The Gresham Press, 1966, *pg 53)*

Edited by Benjamin Durley

ISBN: 979-8-9936869-0-5

Mount Harvard Publishing
(Division of Mount Harvard Press)
Schaumburg, Illinois, USA
For inquiries, reach us at:
office@mountharvardpress.com

TABLE OF CONTENTS

EDITOR'S NOTE

When I think of St. Joseph the Hesychast and Cave-Dweller (+1959) of Little Saint Anne and New Skete on the Holy Mountain, I remember his holiness, his self-denial and his admonitions but also his disappointment because of the prevailing climate in his days regarding noetic prayer. Even older monks, weathered by ascesis and temptations, avoided saying the Jesus Prayer out of fear of falling into delusion. The Saint himself called this the "delusion of the age," prophesying a decline of monastic discipline in these, our last days.

St. Joseph practiced this most sublime of prayers, nonetheless, as did his disciples who subsequently brought it to the "new world," giving even Orthodox Christians in America the possibility to learn the prayer, improving their spiritual lives and bringing them closer in their walk with our Lord.

Noetic prayer is mystical prayer, and it can rightly be called "prayer of the heart." It has always been the prayer of the "poor in spirit" of the Beatitudes, the prayer of the peasant class, a private way of communicating with God Almighty, without prayer books, One-on-one. It is absolutely free of deception, according to St. Joseph, because it abolishes imagination, so that pure prayer can blossom in the heart, allowing man to know Him on a personal level.

We have been blessed with the great gift of access to elders and monks who have dedicated their lives to God through this Prayer and who follow Christ's command to "love thy neighbor" by giving their time and patient guidance to those who desire to learn. When I think of all those who search the world for this knowledge, for a guide to teach them, I am humbled by the thought that I, the greatest of sinners and truly the most unworthy of men, have been granted such access to, and guidance in, this spiritual practice. Should we who have been afforded this great blessing not help ourselves and others who search for such higher things? These holy men, who dedicate their lives to seeking and serving our Lord, generously bestow on us their knowledge and unerringly guide our efforts by their experience and wise counsels, and we must honor their love for us and our Lord's commandment and share this great spiritual treasure to the best of our abilities.

Finally, these dialogues have helped me on my spiritual journey. The guidance and teaching captured herein has changed every aspect of my life and has made me understand in my heart what it is to follow God and to be a true Christian.

Benjamin Durley

PROLOGUE

"Father, if you do this work, you will see miracles in your life."

This is what I was told, not so long ago, by the humble monk presented in these dialogues. The work he was referring to is the work of noetic prayer.

Up until that point, noetic prayer for me, was something far away. It was something obscure, some higher level of spirituality, unavailable to most people. Something to read about, and to hope for someday. This seems to be a common state for many, even for other clergy, and those faithful who are interested in the deeper things of the faith.

Since meeting that monk however, I have been doing the work he has been teaching me to do. Everything has changed. The Cross of the Priesthood is ever present, as it must be, but I have seen, and am seeing, miracles. Miracles of all kinds, in my life, and in the lives of the faithful few God has given me to lead. It is all beyond beautiful. And it is real.

It is like stretching out and breathing fresh air in the sunshine, after toiling for years in some dark, dusty place. It is the real thing that every soul needs, especially in our age of shattered attention, and broken-heartedness; in our culture of make believe.

Noetic prayer is for everyone, lay and monastic alike. The Holy Ones have told us so, but why do we not believe them? Why do we believe instead, those who say, "that's not for us?" What is for us, then?

What do we have, if we do not have noetic prayer? We have much! We have much… that is worth little. Much to talk

1

about. Much that is not helpful. Many facts, quotes, and opinions… theoretical knowledge… distracting us from the fact, that we do not really have empirical knowledge of God. Much, to keep us down in the dusty dark. Much that is not real. A strange fire (*Lev. 10:1-2*).

The "much" must go, for the prayer to come. For the much to go, we must be taught how to let go of it. Who will teach us? Who will teach us to let go of our own distorted images of reality? Who will teach us to pray noetically? Who will give us the work to do? Whose flame will light our own?

Our candles cannot be lit by a computer. A candle must be lit from a living flame. Thank God, he has granted us flame-bearers in the eighth millennium. Whole brotherhoods and sisterhoods of flame-bearers, who have received their fire in succession from the Holy Ones of old, on down through to the spiritual giants of our own time, who have set the table for us.

It is my great joy, an unexpected joy at that, to present these teachings from a humble monk of such a brotherhood. Another thing he told me: "The people need more now." Noetic prayer is "the more." Read these words. Do this work. You will see miracles in your life. Through the prayers of the Elder.

Rev. Father Ephraim Tauck

INTRODUCTION

When Orthodox writers speak about the "descent of the nous to the heart" what meaning do they give to the heart? There are two definitions of the word "heart." In the first instance, it is the fleshy heart which is the control center of our physical being with powers of nurturance, growth, and bodily strength as its attributes. In the second instance, the heart is the spiritual center, the nous. The nous does the thinking, desiring, and acting upon decisions which it alone makes. These physical and spiritual elements coexist, one inside the other, united together until the time of death, when the spirit will return to God and the flesh will go in the grave.

Therefore, the physical heart is the shrine where the nous is found. This place is the actual point of encounter between the human and the divine, since the nous is the image of God and the point where He resides and speaks to man using his conscience, teaching him, censuring him, and guiding him toward His kingdom. The nous begets thoughts and rules over a man's emotions and desires when it is healthy. This nous then, which mainly translates into English as "mind," is the chief organ of intelligence, which is contained in the physical heart and has the power of attention, which it uses to think, feel, and recognize. Thus, nous can also be defined as "attention."

So "to descend down into the heart" or to "return the nous to the heart" is nothing more than to be ATTENTIVE upon the region of the physical heart. This is huge! For through this concentration the powers of the nous unite, and a man is mindful of his higher calling. He becomes aware of spiritual things and senses easily the various evil thoughts and temptations that appear with the purpose of distracting him during prayer. In other words, the attention at the fleshy heart allows the watchfulness, the vigilance, of a spiritual man to kick in.

The purpose of this humble book is to inform those who are looking for something higher, to encourage them, and to protect them from the sirens of disbelief who war against prayer. Hearsay cannot be pitted against real life experience. The actual concept of this most sublime spiritual work, that of noetic prayer, will leave one in awe for its simplicity, so the reader may consider a careful study of this book with a clear mind, void of predisposition. One should also have patience so that the subject matter may be absorbed by the heart. The brain will only reject it. Spiritual things are foolish to a carnal man, as St. Paul the Apostle says, but for a spiritual man they are life. The Jesus Prayer being recited within one's heart is life support, and comfort, especially at this time. It fights idleness and indifference and gives value to our existence in a world without values.

an anonymous hesychast

- The nous is the mind, not the intellect. It is that faculty of the soul that makes a man rational.
- The nous is spirit, and it is found at the physical organ of the heart.
- When one sleeps the nous is in the heart, undivided. As one awakes, a portion of this spirit of nous fills the head, dividing it between the heart and the head.
- The nous at the heart begets thoughts and the nous at the head processes them using the brain and the imagination.
- The spirit of the nous at the heart is defined as "nous essence." The spirit of the nous at the head is defined as "nous energy."
- But the Holy Fathers call the nous at the heart "heart" and the nous at the head "nous." They do this to distinguish between the two.
- The nous at the heart and the nous at the head are of the same substance.
- The nous at the heart is the "inner man" (the thinker). The nous at the head is noetic energy emanating from the "inner man."
- It ascends to the head along with all the thoughts and goes back to the heart when one is asleep to unite with the nous there and to give the brain a rest.
- This also happens during "prayer of the heart." But this time, in a state of absolute wakefulness.
- This movement is called, by hesychasts, the "return of the nous to the heart."

- This happens naturally to all Christians during a moment of tearful repentance.
- But there is also a method to cause this union of the nous to happen, even if contrition of the heart has not yet reached this high level.
- Why should we do this? To have an understanding of the importance of this work, we begin by learning what this nous is that returns and how it works.
- The nous at the head is an energy, as we have mentioned. Four definitions describe its function: consciousness, awareness, attention and focus.
- When one awakes, it comes up from the heart to feel, to be attentive and focused, and to be aware.
- Without some of this "nous energy" at the head, the brain cannot work to process information, and neither can the faculty of the imagination work to help the thinking process.
- This is one of the main reasons why a monk descends with his nous to his heart, to eliminate any distraction during prayer so that the focus stays on prayer and all the mental images are shuffled away. Before descending the nous to the heart, these images are projected on the mind to entice the one praying.
- This is the sublime work of nepsis (watchfulness), when the nous at the head and the nous at the heart come together in unity.
- So, when a thought ascends to the head to be worked over, the imagination "dresses" that thought with an image accordingly, so that the thought may be analyzed, and a decision may be made.

Continued on page 228

THE DIALOGUES, PART 1

A DIALOGUE WITH A MONK ABOUT NOETIC PRAYER - FIRST TALK

Monk) Welcome, my friends, once again to our humble monastery. Come and sit in our meeting room where we will exchange pleasantries and words of encouragement. Today man needs fellowship more than ever... Would you like to share some thoughts of a spiritual nature? Do you have any questions?

Q) Father, we came here to learn. Could you talk to us about the spiritual life?

A) Ahh! You are philosophers, students of wisdom. You see beyond the ephemeral – very good. The here-and-now is short-lived, the curtains are going down, the show and the fanfare will cease to be. Then will the wailing commence, the freezing cold, and the gnashing of teeth, God forbid. We all must avoid this evil.

Q) Would you like to give us some tips on how to avoid going to hell?

A) Firstly, do not think about hell. But only have a faint understanding in the back of your nous as to how it would be to live without Jesus for all eternity. This slight remembrance will be the reins that control behavior. As it is written in Proverbs, "The fear of the Lord is the beginning of wisdom." Not a pathological fear, mind you, but like the door to His Kingdom, which is now open to everyone who repents, a door which will close at some time in the future.

Q) How do we keep this remembrance fresh in our minds?

A) We attend church on Sundays and great feasts, as we are able. We read Holy Scripture, we respect and love our neighbor, we try to do the right thing, and we try to communicate with our Maker. Most Orthodox Christians use for this purpose *"direct prayer"* with supplications and entreaties, with words of joy, and sorrow, with tears of repentance, with a sense of gratitude. And there is also *"spiral prayer"* when by looking at nature one is reminded of Him who created all things from scratch, and one gives thanks. These prayers keep the memory of God alive.

Q) Are there other prayers?

A) There are three kinds of prayer which man often utilizes. The first and second, the "direct" and "spiral" prayers that I mentioned, are based on external perceptions and plenty of intellectual work by using many words in combination with spiritual contemplation. And there is a third type...

Q) Which is?

A) The third form is *"circular,"* which is also called "pure." Way back in time this prayer was the more prevalent form of prayer among the masses; folks back then were more adept at prayer, even more so than the monks of today, although they were illiterate for the most part. They would not, indeed could not, use long fancy words to express themselves. A deep sigh was their prayer, and the repetition of a few inaudible words blended in with their tears.

Q) What happened to those days, Father?

A) St. Gregory Palamas wrote much in favor of mystical prayer and, being himself an expert, among the greatest monastics of all time, he prepared a model for us to follow to get back home praying like we should. "Circular" prayer is the answer.

During this prayer the nous leaves the externals and the many words and "returns to itself."

Q) What do you mean by "returns to itself"?

A) When you love someone, you do not say a whole lot, you go by feeling and emotion. Direct and spiral prayers need the active use of our brains and, therefore, they are not totally free of deception. During these meditations many have fallen into heresies. Demonic entry is not impossible considering that fantasy takes a part, even in a minimal way. But during circular prayer intellectual activity ceases. Therefore, fantasy is obliterated, and the soul unites into a whole.

Q) Say that again?

A) The nous is always busy bringing our awareness to thoughts, ideas and stimuli. As such, it usually scatters to the "outside" and we must bring it back to its source, our heart, by focused attention and willpower. Prayer is our objective as Christians: to put our heart in it, to pray undistractedly.

Q) What really is the heart?

A) It is our spiritual heart or what is called "nous". The nous has desire, cognition, and volition. These are the three aspects or powers of the soul and the image of God in man. When we desire something, our cognition (or power of intelligence) produces analogous thoughts, uses the brain to evaluate and to process them, and our will power struggles to bring our decisions into fruition.

Q) Where is this nous, or spiritual heart, located?

A) It is found in our physical heart, but it is deep. The Holy Fathers call the heart an immeasurable abyss. Our passions are also there with the roots of all our senses, and it is a natural, paranatural and supernatural center.

Q) Can you elaborate on this?

A) The heart can feel the physical and spiritual realities with the senses akin to each. And it is a natural center by which man lives his life now, after the fall of the protoplasts, according to his nature; a paranatural center with all the blasphemous tendencies, appetites and generally all the vices that push one to do unnatural things, and a supernatural center into whose depths the Spirit of God enters by Baptism. Since we have God inside of us, we have the ability to live in a state above our nature.

Q) Can you tell us more about the *"nous"*? What is it?

A) The mind. This is the word that best conveys the meaning of the word nous. The nous constitutes the inner man. It begets thoughts consciously. It is also called "the eye of the soul" by which we become aware and communicate with our Creator. So, the nous is the faculty of thought, and it has consciousness, awareness, attention, focus – definitions Greeks also use when they are referring to nous.

Q) What about undistractedness?

A) It means to pray with all we have got. This is the great Commandment given in Matthew 22:37: to love the Lord with all our heart, our soul, and our mind. These are the three powers we just mentioned and circular prayer brings them together. This prayer is also called *"noetic"* or *"prayer of the heart"*.

Q) Tell us more about it, will you?

A) Noetic prayer is the most wonderful and sublime activity of the human mind. This is so because we use the Name of Jesus, before which all knees shall bow. The Jesus Prayer, "Lord Jesus Christ have mercy on me," contains the divine Name, and thus it becomes the conduit of God's grace and all other heavenly gifts. From my understanding, the Lord's Name is God's gift to humanity.

Q) You have mentioned fantasy, what about it?

A) You all know that in order to break through the clouds of distraction, so to taste the joyful and cleansing effect of prayer, the fantasies and imaginations must cease to operate so as not to provoke the passions, for the imagination is used by the devil to lead man to sin.

Q) Please continue?

A) Back in the day, the people were virtuous and smart. They protected themselves and the eyes of their children from indecent imagery. Also, they did not entice each other with improper dress and attitude. Therefore, their memory was unsoiled. One could see this from their countenance and their whole demeanor. Today, this great wall of values has been torn down, mainly by the use of technology and media. And the impressions that are amassed through one's life make it difficult to keep the mind clear during church, at work, or even during other essential pastimes. The constant influx of stimuli and impressions, along with the memories they create, fuel imagination and fantasies, which are "the bridge of the devil".

Q) This is true. But what can we do now?

A) Let me explain. After the fall of Adam, man thinks with images. Thoughts come up to the head from the heart and are manifested as pictures. A pious Orthodox Christian is called to reject the proposals of the sinful variety of images. It starts from here, with the use of the Jesus Prayer and watchfulness, diligently rejecting sin until it becomes a good habit.

Q) What is watchfulness?

A) Since you are somewhat learned, but with humility you approach this subject of prayer, I will answer this way: watchfulness is unceasing vigilance whereby we watch inwardly to expel any thoughts coming our way.

11

Q) You talked about impressions. How can we systematically improve?

A) You will improve immediately by living simply. Being a monk, I cannot be attached to "things of the world". God is first and foremost. This is a good example. So, listen: a monk cannot play video games or have Internet. He cannot watch TV or have an iPhone. He cannot see a movie or read the news. It is out of the question. I cannot be hooked to material things precisely because of impressions. To pray noetically, as my elder suggested, I have to have in mind the Jesus Prayer, and only that.

Q) Interesting. But how are you able to have only the Jesus Prayer in mind now, while you speak with us?

A) Have you noticed that I always take control of our conversations? What will I gain from talking about other people, the weather, the war, politics, and what have you? Now we are talking about noetic prayer and my attention is on this topic, watchfulness and prayer for a monk are perpetual, a way of life, do you follow?

Q) We understand. But is memory a bad thing?

A) You know the answer, though you are testing me. So be it. The evil one uses all the "trash" stored in our memory to keep us busy. And when we sit or stand to pray, he tempts us with this or that thought from the past or with something we saw recently to stop us from focusing on communion with God.

Q) I have read about the famous *"noetic prayer"* can you elaborate on this?

A) I will. But I must insist that you take baby steps first. Simply say the prayer: "Lord Jesus Christ have mercy on me" and listen intently to the holy words as you pronounce them. After a time, you will want to repeat it often, because it gladdens the soul. If you tire out, put the prayer in motion with your lips so your mind can take a breather. Saying it mechanically is good too, even if you do not understand what you are saying. The devil hears, though, and he freaks out. Of course, it is best when we are attentive and completely focused on prayer but what can one do when he must work and has to think? Oral prayer, even if "mechanical," is good for those times when we cannot be 100% in prayer.

Q) Will this prayer, said orally, bring on clear-headedness?

A) Not in the full sense of the word. But it can stand as guard when we are assaulted by a bad thought, to remind us that we do not play with this sort of game, with reverie and daydreaming, and *"coupling"* with an enemy who wants to devour us.

Q) What do you mean by coupling?

A) Coupling is the second stage of sin, when a man entertains the "assault" instead of rejecting it. If he talks to and entertains it, then he most likely will accept the sinful offer and fall into the sin, because the devil has the power of persuasion. So, when the Jesus Prayer is repeated often enough, the grace that it attracts will automatically serve as a shield to protect and enlighten us to act.

Q) You said coupling is the "second stage" and mention "the assault;" what are the other stages?

A) We speak in terms of four stages of sin. The first is the "assault," wherein a memory or thought strikes us, or is presented to us, to tempt us. The second is "coupling" or "entertaining it," wherein we contemplate the thought and where we become comfortable with the idea. The third stage is "the fall;" this is committing the actual sin itself, which becomes almost inevitable if we allow ourselves to couple with the thoughts. The fourth stage is "passion" where, after

13

falling into the same sin repeatedly we find ourselves less and less able to resist: our sin becomes a habit we can't break.

Q) So, we can either reject or accept a thought; what else can we do to prevent "coupling"?

A) There is another way to handle thoughts, and that is to not allow them to become images up in the head. Our Lord disclosed to us in His gospel that all iniquity comes from the heart: murder, adultery... and we are assaulted constantly. Of course, most evil we do not want. The devil uses subtleties to fool us, and we willingly cooperate, so that we often do not even recognize evil.

Q) Is that so?

A) Yes, as a matter of fact, most thoughts are not even ours. As St. Diadochos has noted: Satan is at the surface and around the heart, smoking up our nous through the desires and pleasures of the flesh. Thus, he is able to project through our inner voice (or logos) all the passionate thoughts. Then, they arise to the head and become conceptual images. Our *fantastico* (imagination or fantasy) plays a key role in this.

Q) The culprit is the imagination, isn't it?

A) Yes, it is. A great elder wrote that the first evil and passionate thought, but primarily the corresponding fantasy, is the starting point of all sin. Sin does not occur indeed if an evil thought does not precede it by means of the imagination.

Q) Hmm! How important is it to know this?

A) Very important! The devils fight us tooth and nail with pictures, pictures, pictures and vivid descriptions, ugly drawings, unbelievable scenes, portraits, pictorials, imaginings, scenic rides, etc., non-stop! Just to have us fall so they can laugh. Man has somewhere around 12,000 thoughts each day, on the average. Each thought carries along an associated image. It is crucial to know that evil thoughts

14

are not ours so that we can ward them off more quickly and not go into guilt trips when we fall.

Q) Father, you said we should not go into guilt trips when we fall to sin; should we not feel guilty?

A) Of course, there will be guilt associated with falling to sin, but we have a proper Christian way of dealing with that: confession, repentance, prayer, and communion.

Q) But the feeling of guilt is still proper and useful for this, right?

A) Yes… but only to the point that it brings us to confession and repentance. Beyond that, we are falling victim to a spiritual attack.

Q) When you say, "spiritual attack", is that like the first stage of sin you told us about; "the assault"?

A) Yes, spiritual attacks generally come in the form of the initial "assault" that tempts us toward sin and they can be quite sneaky and unrelenting! Satan knows where we are weak and tempts us continually by introducing the thoughts and images that play to our weaknesses. It is important to recognize how such attacks come in order to maintain watchfulness.

Q) Father, can you tell us more about how we can recognize these attacks?

A) Think of these attacks coming from one of six directions. The "guilt trip" we discussed is a "downward" or "down" attack: the devil throws us down into a feeling of despair and worthlessness beyond that which spurs us into repentance. In this attack, we can become dejected and apathetic and lose our spiritual connection if we are not watchful. The opposite of the "down" attack is the "up" or "upward", which takes the form of excessive zeal.

Q) But zeal is a good thing, isn't it?

A) Yes, and so is regret for sins, but not when carried to extremes. In an "up" attack, we are tempted to immerse ourselves too deeply, too quickly in the spiritual arts which can result in spiritual burnout, even threatening our faith. Proverbs warns us about this one: "When you find honey, eat what is sufficient, lest being filled, you should vomit it up."

Q) So, after up and down, what is next?

A) The next attack is "from the left" and it is easily recognized; it brings the temptations of our clearly sinful passions, such as: lust, envy, anger, etc. Then comes the attack "from the right," which is trickier: it fools us into thinking we are doing something "right" and good for the love of God but, in reality, we are motivated by pride or a desire to feel important. This can be commonly seen in new Christians already seeing themselves in positions of power in the church, such as becoming clergy, ministry heads, etc., even before they have become properly Christian.

Q) And then?

A) The last two are the attack "from the front" and the attack "from the back." The attack "from the front" takes the form of excessive worry about the future rather than trusting in the Lord or daydreaming about the future, possibly developing plans and giving-in to material and worldly focus. The attack "from the back" keeps us stuck in the past. We cannot shake the memories of past sins, temptations, or events that continue to cause us to struggle with our faith or faithfulness.

Q) Do all attacks come from these directions?

A) You are intelligent people, and I am sure you can see that these are guidelines more than scientific facts. That said, most every attack that comes can be associated with one of these "directions of spiritual attack".

Q) Why is it important to know this?

A) We must remember that the devil is extremely clever and very persistent. He is always looking for ways to separate us from our Lord. His attacks are subtle and well-disguised, and he often hits us with combination attacks. Understanding the direction of these attacks helps us see through the deception and recognize the attacks. This supports our watchfulness and helps us to resist!

Q) Back to the initial "assault": my brain produces pictorials all day long; does that mean that I will perish?

A) Do not worry so much. There is a way to train the nous, where it is slowly cleansed and, by extension, the heart is also systematically cleansed. This method prevents imagery from occurring. Not always but in increments of a few minutes each day. You are not monks. You still have to live in the world, in chaos. Still, in time and with diligence, this ideal will happen.

Q) Please do continue, Father, will you?

A) The method is "hesychasm" by which a man's heart comes into stillness: undisturbed, that is, and freed from thoughts, passions, imaginings, and from influences of the environment.

Q) Does this method entail prayer of the heart?

A) I'd say that you are familiar with hesychasm. Yes. It is most definitely connected with the prayer of the heart, the circular, noetic, or pure prayer. Now, before I go on, I must say that there are presuppositions to go along with this prayer, such as: being Orthodox, having a father-confessor, honoring thy parents. You all know this. You are educated. One or two among you might even become priests to serve a parish.

Q) By the way, Father, can we say the Jesus Prayer in church?

A) Let me guess: you are concerned that the Divine Liturgy is communal prayer, as they say, but the Jesus Prayer is private, is that right? Let me tell you something: The Jesus Prayer is whispered in the bosom of a simple monk going round and round, constantly. So, will he stop it? No. With the name of Jesus being recited especially during the Divine Liturgy, the atmosphere does not get any more communal than that, or grace filled. At precisely this time, when a man calls on Jesus during the liturgy, he may find that he becomes part of the sacrament, so therefore when we talk about the prayer, it is good to have discernment.

Q) Can I ask, what is discernment?

A) There is a need for discernment in all levels of life. Everyone learns how to discern, to judge, to recognize, to discriminate, to apply common sense. In friendships, marriage, educational decisions, occupations, propositions, wrong or proper etiquette. In discernment of a spiritual kind, a decision is connected to the afterlife. Heaven or Hell is at stake. Therefore, it is good to be prudent.

Q) Father, now that you mentioned the priesthood, is noetic prayer suited for the parish priest?

A) Most definitely. The mystical prayers articulated inside of us have great value. St. Gregory of Sinai, in the Philokalia, said "we are all called to carry the law of the Spirit written on the tablets of our hearts, and to attain like the Cherubim the supreme privilege of conversing through pure prayer in the heart directly with Jesus." The prayer is for us all! Our predecessors could barely read. They prayed silently using their own words, or the Jesus Prayer, and the prayers to the Theotokos... How much more appropriate, then, is it for our spiritual leaders, our pastors and shepherds, to "carry the law of the Spirit" in their hearts?

Q) My grandpa was like that, isn't it funny?

A) When they were all fired-up, their nous rendered ineffable cries and entreaties personally to the Lord. And they were illumined. They were simple folks, farmers, smiths, and well-diggers. So, this is hesychasm, the mystery of union between Almighty God and little, insignificant man, with prayer of the heart, with tears, with repentance, One-on-one with God.

Q) Does intelligence help prayer at all?

A) Cultivating the intellect is not necessary. True knowledge does not come by reason but by grace when it finds the heart pure. Intelligence cannot ensure salvation, nor can it help at all to ward off evil coming around. Without divine help, darkness reigns in one's soul, regardless of his smarts and wit.

Q) How is prayer of the heart applied?

A) The nous returns to itself, as we have discussed. St. Theophan the Recluse calls it "the descent of the mind into the heart". There is a simple technique to help the nous go down to the heart. I will show you.

Q) Forgive me, is this truly for everyone?

A) Yes, it is for everyone but, as I mentioned, there are prerequisites to be ready and capable of noetic prayer. We have a good group here. I know all of you personally. For those who are very proud and cannot impede the advance of their imaginations, however innocent they seem to be, I have to say this: they will be deceived no matter what, even by saying the Lord's prayer or just by reading a book.

Q) Could you continue?

A) Let me simplify noetic prayer. So, the nous is our awareness, our attention, our focus. When we subtract our focus from the head (not all of it) and we put it on our physical organ of the heart, in our chest, that is when we feel our heart, then imagination stops. The faculty of imagination is up in our brain but in order to produce and promote its images, it needs awareness. The nous must be there, our awareness, that is. When we have captured the nous in our heart, the office is closed; there are no pictures.

Q) How clever. Isn't it?

A) I dare to say that man can stay sinless even for these few minutes during the prayer of the heart. The method is so innocent and simple and yet so misunderstood by our community, at large. The people are misinformed.

Q) Did I hear something negative on YouTube about noetic prayer?

A) I have heard it said that there is a lack of respect for inner prayer among some of those who preach online. There has even come to view unjustifiable slander against one of St. Nicodemos's greatest achievements, the Philokalia. "Do not read the Philokalia, I do not even read the Philokalia!" said one such "expert," insinuating that the contents of this exceptional book can do harm to those who read it. One must be discerning; not everyone who offers opinions has actual expertise on the subject.

Q) This is strange, father. Now... can you complete your talk of presuppositions?

A) Well, there is self-reliance, the biggest evil. We must battle with this. We must listen to our elders or priests. Man had inherited self-reliance in the garden of Eden, from then on, he has this conviction that he can do things himself, that he knows better. He is sometimes snobbish, conceited, and disobedient. The ones who rely on themselves are toys for the dark spirits. But for those who ask with humility what to do, devilish schemes will not work against them. Also, fantasies cannot prevail when pitted against a simple and humble mind. Really! What strength of spirit God has bestowed on his people!

Q) What about our conscience?

A) Our conscience is God's voice. But we cannot always be certain that it is His voice that speaks. There is also the so-called "evil conscience" which often comes with the pretense of good, yet in essence it is evil. According to St. Gregory of Sinai every beginner possesses two forms of energy: good energy and bad energy, and the beginner cannot tell the difference between them.

Q) How can we distinguish between these energies?

A) Go to confession. I will tell you this very significant detail from the life of my brothers. The serious novice, rassophore, or great-schema monk does not wait to fall into sin so he can go afterward to confession. An experienced monk "sees" trouble from afar and reveals it to his elder without waiting, before thoughts fester. So, he stays clean. This also destroys self-reliance and builds humility! Do you understand?

Q) How could we have known this?

A) If you had visited, talked to, and listened to a man of God, even like the simple apprentice monk who tills the garden wearing a tattered cassock, with dirt under his boots, then you would know. So, as I was saying, it is a prerequisite to learn prayer while having someone to go to, to reveal your shortcomings, your thoughts, everything, quickly.

Q) What books on prayer are good to read?

A) Start with "The Way of the Pilgrim." The unknown author of this awesome little book must be a saint. Again, as we said earlier, put the mouth in motion as did "the pilgrim". Call out this wonderful name day and night if you have to. The quantity of the Jesus Prayer invoked, opens the heart to receive and enthrone Christ within. The apostle Paul urged us to pray unceasingly.

Q) I would like to ask something. Could I use a prayer rope?

A) Of course. Now, the use of a prayer rope serves two reasons. For one, we count by the knots the number of prayers so to fulfill our monastic everyday rule. Also, we use a prayer rope to attract our attention down to our hand and away from our head so that we will not have as many thoughts and images.

Q) I didn't know that. Is there more to this?

A) A few minutes ago, I simplified noetic prayer and I said the same things as for the prayer rope, except that we attract our focus/attention to the heart instead of the hand. The idea is very simple: we use focus and sensation to keep the attention, our nous, away from our heads. But, to have better success in any prayer, as I have said, our thoughts must be revealed and not kept secret in our heads and hearts. We begin there to help inner prayer.

Q) Father, why is it so hard to curtail passionate thoughts?

A) We have strength of spirit. We are created free and rational, and we are endowed with the power to say no to sin since our power is equal to the demons' attacking force. But our soul wins or loses according to its inclination toward that which the demon presents. So, the scale leans in his favor, you see, because of our hearts' sympathy toward that particular temptation: captivity then, can happen quickly as it depends on how much we desire a certain passion.

Q) But why does it feel good to sin?

A) Good question. The dreadful consent and yielding of the soul to a sinful idea which has been presented to it is, oftentimes, accompanied by delight. This happened to the first people before eating the forbidden fruit. As was their case, we are also delighted when committing a sin, that which is conscientiously forbidden.

Q) But then comes bitterness, does it not?

A) Surely. Just like it happened in Paradise after the disobedience. Remember when we touched upon the issue of coupling or entertaining thoughts? This is death. So once again, revelation of thoughts to a confessor is equally important to prayer, if not superior in significance. When we engage with a demonic provocation, instead of renouncing it, a sensually intense feeling arouses our interest for the sinful suggestion. Then our communication with God comes to a halt. This happens often and happens even more often to those who think highly of themselves as humility is essential to prayer. And then as sin is being committed, the sensual intensity goes up a notch or two. The result is bitterness and resentment.

Q) So, are you going back to watchfulness?

A) Watchfulness, or nepsis, as the Greek fathers call it, helps to curtail the passions by confessing sins before they happen. When my nous stands guard at the gate of my heart, as soon as something appears like a whim, an impulse, an urge or a memory which might stir up an evil desire in me in the near future, I run to my elder. My success in prayer, as I have noted, is the revelation of my heart's offspring. Still, a prayerful mind warns me in time.

Q) But are you, Father, still in danger of sinful desire?

A) The ancients used to say, "know thyself". I carry, as we all do, the primordial fall of our first parents. When they were created, the image of God in them was intact, now it is fragmented. We are all a mess.

Q) Did you not say in the very beginning that with circular prayer the soul unites?

A) Sure. If I want it badly enough. And for success in all endeavors the soul unites. If we do anything in life and we want to excel in it, we must desire it with all our heart, we must have all our mind on it, and we should strive to make it happen with all our effort. As for me, perfection has not been easy. I am still working on it.

Q) Didn't St. Gregory Palamas write about this?

A) Yes. Man's soul which is the image of the Holy Trinity unites with the prototype. Until then? Does modern man have the strength to deny a sinful living? There are so many demonic attacks and he is bewildered as to how to unite his soul. Amazing!

Q) I too want to ask something. Tell us, please, a minute ago you said that you are "working on it"; what do you do?

A) Not much. I do my obedience and I try to have patience. I keep in mind that pain and suffering is our lot here on earth. Our first parents ate from the tree of pleasure and pain and today since sensual pleasures have taken over the world, pain creeps in to balance things out. There is no avoiding hardships, troubles, sorrow, diseases, misfortunes, temptations, and grief. St. Joseph the Hesychast says that "pain is the antidote to sensual-sinful pleasure. Pain and suffering cleanse the Soul."

Q) Pain and suffering...?

A) I do not look for them. But I know they're coming. I do not want surprises, so I made up my mind that such adversity is around the corner. Henceforth I found peace. Mankind is suffering as we speak. Why should I be an exception?

Q) What about your prayer life?

A) That is what I am driving at. As a monk, I like to serve as your example. When you have patience and thank God for all things, good and bad, then prayer comes very easy. It attaches to the heart. A strong prayer becomes a necessity when our volition, our will power, is pushed to a certain limit, depending on Divine providence. So relentless tribulation is a key element to prayer of the heart when utilized in accordance with His laws. Our part in this is patience and discernment. Then perfection is realized. After many difficulties the heart is conditioned to apprehend lofty spiritual states, and finally dispassion.

Q) In other words, "no pain, no gain," right?

A) I guess. Now, for you boys, there is no need to worry. If you do what your spiritual father tells you, you'll be fine. After all, your leash is long. Your focus should be on the commandments. Well, obedience cannot hurt but... it all depends on your endurance.

Q) Regarding our spiritual guide, what is required of him?

A) Humility and know-how. A good man traditionally recognizes his strengths and his limitations. For practical everyday issues, the shepherd there at your parish should be your "go to", but when you consider being adept at prayer on a higher level, he should respect your position and not hinder you from seeking more in-depth guidance, when needed.

Q) What should we say to those who believe this higher spiritual standard is not for us?

A) Firstly, we must understand that there are well-meaning but misinformed people throughout the church who think that there is no need for us to pursue this higher spiritual standard. And there are others who simply are not adept at prayer and, therefore, see reaching a higher level as unavailable to the regular Christian. But right after Jesus told us that we must take up our cross and follow Him, He warned us that doing so would lead to divisions. This is all about deepening our relationship with God and each man's journey is between him and God alone. I would say to those who truly thirst for more, they should seek a guide and "go and search to learn more, for your own benefit."

Q) Oh, Father, do you know how thirsty we are?

A) I promised to show you something. It is basic but, at the same time, advanced; now is a good time. So, quantity brings quality. After quite a while of saying the Jesus Prayer orally, "Lord Jesus Christ have mercy on me," while paying attention to the holy words pronounced, you will begin to recite the prayer inside of you, silently. Try that.

Q) Ok... but at what pace?

A) Say it comfortably. Have the words of the prayer adhere to your breath. When breathing in say "Lord Jesus Christ" and when breathing out say "have mercy on me". Or say one whole prayer when breathing in and the whole prayer while breathing out. Use whichever rhythm works best for you. So, by pulling the prayer into the lung area with the breath and pushing it out again with the breath, the breath and the Jesus Prayer unite and travel together.

Q) It makes sense. Are we to say it inwardly?

A) That's right. You will give the breath the prayer to repeat as it is moving along out of the chest and then back in. By doing this the Jesus Prayer and breath become one and, since the breath is automatic and always going on of its own accord, when the Jesus Prayer adheres to the breath, the prayer also becomes automatic and, by God's grace, it will continue to go on its own.

Q) Father, I am already hearing the prayer going on while I breathe. Am I losing it?

A) No. This is nothing strange or mysterious. It happens to everyone after being in a store shopping, or at the supermarket, haven't you noticed this? You come home and the songs you heard are playing in your head. When the mind picks up something pleasing it repeats it. More so in your case as the prayer has attached to your breath.

Q) Can this prayer be called unceasing?

A) Call it what you want; unceasing, continuous, or self-acting. This prayer has beauty unrivaled by all other means of prayer because it carries the name Jesus which is above all names. With this Name the saints raised the dead.

Q) I am also saying the prayer now within me, could tell us more about this phenomenon?

A) The action of the Holy Spirit propels the prayer. No one can call upon the Name of Jesus on his own. In our monasteries this memorable experience is not at all uncommon. It happens to serious pilgrims who come from far away with zeal and with God in their hearts, having been baptized in the name of the Holy Trinity. Once a pious man came to visit who spoke only English. After sharing a meal with us in the refectory and participating in vespers, he spent the night in our guesthouse. In the morning, as he woke up, he clearly heard the Jesus player being repeated inside his head – not in English – but in Greek! Isn't that something?

Q) In Greek?

A) Not that a language matters; I just made this incident known to point out that the man's inner voice acted involuntarily. This is the only time I have heard about in which the prayer has played out within a mind in a foreign tongue. Yet, the prayer's holy words resounding endlessly within, are the bread and butter for those who occupy their time saying it, no matter in which language. It is true that noetic prayer can become impulsive for the heart moves endlessly, and so does the prayer.

Q) Even at night?

A) Definitely. Monks only sleep three to four hours at a time, and they are always praying. It's a hard life but the Jesus Prayer must go on to nourish and then protect a soul when the body rests. We have to be on the alert 24/7.

Q) You are alert always?

A) I cannot lie to you. Nepsis, watchfulness, relies heavily on the nous (which is found in the depths of our being) to do its work. The nous is the "eye of the soul," as I have mentioned earlier. It has awareness of itself and its surroundings. It can see, feel, and recognize noetic concepts that are otherwise incomprehensible to the faculty of reason. The more prayer we give to the nous the more attuned and aware it becomes and the more able to sense, to encounter, and to successfully confront demonic provocations. Since a monk is always very cautious, the operation of his watchfulness/vigilance becomes, in time, second nature. That is, for the nous to be always on guard.

Q) Can you give us an idea how vigilance works during sleep?

A) I cannot really expound on this idea, but neither would you understand if I did. Let me try, nonetheless, to form an outline by which you may grasp the concept of keeping the mind pure during the night hours. The desire of the heart must surrender completely to God. And the nous and the will must surrender to this pious desire; then the soul unites in agreement and vigilance cannot be interrupted.

Q) Come again?

A) Remember in the beginning we touched upon the three powers of the soul (desire, intelligence and volition)? Well, if the heart desires purity during sleep and the intelligence agrees and looks out for trouble, then the volition (strength of will) helps to fulfill that desire. In other words, "where there is a will there is a way". If you want it, think about it, and it shall happen.

Q) What about dreams?

A) Never pay attention to dreams, the elders tell us. You are not liable for whatever happens during a dream. During sleep the nous, which is our consciousness and our awareness, nestles in its home in the heart, which allows any thought that drifts aimlessly to ascend up to the head but, since our nous is not there to pay attention to it, the brain cannot function fully and does not know what to make of these thoughts.

Q) Let me ask a stupid question, Father: why are we not liable?

A) During a deep sleep we are unconscious and, therefore, we are not responsible if a bad thought enters the scope of our spiritual eyesight. While we are conscious, since we are created free and rational, we choose consciously to sin or not. Of course, the unconscious mind cannot make such rational decisions. But listen: if during this time we become half-awake, from then on, we must be careful. At that time, when inappropriate images are forming as we are between sleep and awake, consciousness begins to build and accountability creeps in. Do you understand?

Q) I think so. But what can we do then?

A) Being half-asleep during prayer is not good. This phase promotes unrestrained demonic activity. What you can do when you notice this state is to break it up by any number of means. Go drink a glass of water. Change your position. Stand up, raise your hands and pray orally. Squeeze your prayer rope or feel the back of your shoulder with your nous/attention. Or, if you are brave, continue to pray noetically and the grace of God might eliminate the fantasy.

Q) Could it be that easy?

A) Of course. As I have said, you can also feel the prayer rope to focus your attention and draw your nous away from fantasy or distraction. This is only one of many timeless principles based on experience. To be sure, the procedures which are to follow are based on these easy little things, in order to shield the mind from injury, these tactics are "tricks of the trade," you could say. The desert father or Athonite ascetic is like any skillful technician: they have the know-how to get the job done.

Q) Father, so far, I am awe-struck by the simplicity of what you are saying. Why do they put fear into us?

A) Let me explain. Watchfulness, the science of the Neptic fathers, is a highly developed branch of spirituality. And it is simple when taught properly. This system includes circular prayer and simple techniques such as these but, because it does require a guide to learn successfully, it's not generally available to the public. This intimidates the uninitiated, and they spread rumors. But please forgive me, it is time to eat. We will continue this conversation after our meal.

Continued on page 75

IN RUSSIA- A TRIP TO VALAAM

Pilgrim) Your blessing, Starets. Can you find some time to speak to us? Please tell us something. We have come from America.

Monk) Of course my children, I shall do that. Come... have a seat all around here. What can I, a simple person, do for you?

Pilgrim) On the boat yesterday we were going over this scholarly work we had read - on watchfulness. Could you elaborate on your understanding of this subject?

Monk) The watchfulness over one's thoughts is a science. It is the guarding of the heart, the struggle not to give in to intrusive thoughts. Without this work a man just keeps falling into the same sins. But there are things you can do to prepare yourselves so that when the warfare begins you will be ready to ward off the evils.

Pilgrim) Does asceticism play a part in this? And if so, what can we do to help ourselves?

Monk) You start by fasting on the designated days and as prescribed by our Church. You have probably noticed that during those times the images formed in the mind to entice us to sin are not so many or as strong as when you are eating meats and other rich and delicious foods.

Pilgrim) I have noticed this myself. Why is that, do you think?

Monk) You are men, and you will not keep your fantasy at bay concerning the passion of lust if you consume various delicacies and cakes, fried foods, that sort of thing. The sensual pleasure derived from them will transfer to and will fuel beastly instincts. Gluttony produces improper scenarios where someone says to himself: "where did that come from?" So, I would implore you to fast, especially the day before receiving Holy Communion.

Pilgrim) But Saturdays, because of our Lord's Resurrection, are fast-free. Isn't that right?

Monk) Nice try. Take it easy with the beef, the chops and dairy products, is what I'm saying. You are not going to perish, trust me. Our predecessors survived the gulag on daily bread. You see, the devil uses delight to attract the soul, and since all sin is connected to sensual pleasure, this is his main weapon along with the fantasy. As soon as we are assaulted with an evil thought, delight is kindled in our heart to make us succumb and accept the offer he is presenting. Therefore, asceticism helps to reduce the heart's love for pleasure, sensually speaking. Because there is also divine pleasure.

Pilgrim) We must try then, to eat simple foodstuffs. I think we all agree. What else can we try, to be able to limit incitement?

Monk) Cultivate the fear of God, which is the fire that melts wicked thoughts. This fear is a gift from God. It will help you struggle to stay "clean" before the face of the Lord who watches over all of his creatures and cares for them. Monastics have this ongoing fear lit all throughout the day and night. You can all try this on for size because I see that you are pious. I also feel that you are educated, and well-read.

Pilgrim) We try. We read a lot from the early Saints and the holy neptic fathers like St. Gregory Palamas and others.

Monk) So do I. You must be familiar with noetic prayer then, the pure prayer, or circular as they call it. I want you to know that this prayer enhances the whole endeavor of watchfulness that you've mentioned.

Pilgrim) Speaking for all of us, it seems that for a modern-day Christian, comprehension of this discipline is beyond his reach.

Monk) Almost. You do understand that we live in the end times. In this age you are most likely to find a starets before a wide screen preparing for a lecture or writing a book of some sort: for prayer, nothing! They think prayer is something outdated. Don't you talk about miracles, they will think that you are mad. And if you cry in Church out of love for God - oh - you must have problems at home. In the days of old we had the saints of Holy Rus' and St. Seraphim Sarovsky, the Optina elders, St. John of Kronstadt... But still, even today you can find a teacher. Maybe not of such stature but holy enough. So, a man can find something if he searches diligently.

Pilgrim) You are saying that one who wants to pray noetically, that he must have guidance?

Monk) Precisely. This renowned prayer cannot be found by reading some books. It is passed on from mentor to pupil and it is very special, indeed, because it helps the mind do away with fantasy. With God's help and some solid instruction, evil imagery will not appear to disturb a praying man. Notice how

32

when the time comes for prayer hell breaks loose with all kinds of unbelievable stories and ideas materializing before your eyes and trying to grab on to mess you up?

Pilgrim) Starets, about the mind, or nous as they call it, what is it exactly? There is confusion concerning the nature of this term and of noetic prayer itself.

Monk) The whole concept of noetic prayer or prayer of the heart is not as complex as it may seem, and so the term nous is the mind - not the brain - but the rational faculty by which we figure things out and think logically as human beings. The nous is spirit, and it is contained within a man's physical heart. This spirit is the eye of the soul, and it is endowed with the ability to see God...

Pilgrim) Forgive me. Your words brought to my mind the Beatitudes just now. Is there a connection here?

Monk) Yes. Our Lord disclosed to us that blessed are those who have a pure heart for they shall see God. In the gospels and throughout Patristic literature the terms "nous" and "heart" are interchangeable, they mean the same thing. The nous is also called "heart" because it is situated in the physical heart. We are urged to cleanse our nous/heart of all iniquity. To the Saints who purified themselves, it was given the ability to see God, each by his own measure. They were successful because of a strong resolve, but not only that: they had the Jesus Prayer in their heart, that is, "Lord Jesus Christ have mercy on me."

Pilgrim) In the Philokalia and relevant books on this Jesus Prayer in the heart, we read about the descent of the nous down to the heart. Could you explain this?

Monk) This movement of the nous to the heart is what eliminates distractions during the time we spend before the Lord begging for mercy. This is an amazingly simple but very effective way to block evil thoughts, which the nous begets in our hearts, from ascending to the head. Now, a question arises: the nous is found in the physical heart, so how will it descend to the heart when it is already down there? And the answer is this: There are two different definitions of nous. There is the nous, the eye of the soul, or inner man who is in the heart producing all kinds of evil as well as wholesome thoughts, and there is the other definition of nous which means attention, or awareness, or focus one could say...

Pilgrim) Hmm, now it starts making sense. But please continue.

Monk) Greek people often use the second definition for nous every day. "Have your nous there," "where is your nous?", they say to denote attention/focus. So therefore the Holy Fathers, who wrote about this mental prayer or prayer of the nous in that particular language, did not feel the need to explain something that was to them self-evident. To have the nous at their heart meant to be aware of the physical heart, to be attentive to that place, to be focused there, to feel their heart.

Pilgrim) This is very simple, Father. Do you know how many years we have been struggling with this enigma? But now, do show us how to be focused down here at our heart, how to feel our heart.

Monk) You will breathe into your chest and stop... there. Where the breath ends, this is where the heart is, the general area around the heart. This cavity is where you want your concentration to be. So, breathe in again, stop and survey this place. Now do this one more time and as you inhale bring your nous/attention inside you along with the air, and trap it in confinement. Then breathe out. Don't let your nous come out as you exhale. This is the idea: to bring the nous inside the chest with your lungs and leave it there in that cavity as you breathe out.

34

Pilgrim) So this is what the Saints refer to when they say, "put your nous in your heart"?

Monk) Exactly. But now, after securing the nous somewhere by the heart or in the near vicinity, one must rhythmically begin to recite the Jesus prayer, but internally, with the inner voice. When doing this, the watchfulness comes of age where the person praying is in control of his thoughts and quickly puts them away before they show up as conceptual images at the head to provoke and then corrupt the soul.

Pilgrim) Christ said that evil thoughts come out of the heart. But we decide whether or not to espouse these thoughts. Even if thoughts appear, we still have the last say. Isn't that correct?

Monk) Listen to me carefully. If you do not abolish an evil idea, desire, notion or concept at its birth, believing that you have the strength and know-how to fight against it afterwards, you will be disappointed. Of course, you have the last say but by that time you will have been crushed. Demons have the power of persuasion. If you let them into your brain - in seconds - they can have you believe that you're a prophet, or a sage of some sort. And the anger, jealousy, dejection, despair, and filth that might rise to head level does not go away quickly. The unbelievable scenes that fantasy might produce will have your head spinning. No, my children. Do not wait but strike them down as soon as they manifest as simple thoughts at the heart, before they take root.

Pilgrim) How is this possible to do it so quickly and easily?

Monk) The kind of vigilance I am talking about requires no peeking by the mind's eye - the nous - to see if a thought is good or bad but to reject ALL thoughts. I know, it sounds strange, but this is noetic prayer when we reject every concept except: "Lord Jesus Christ have mercy on me." A smart one might ask: "what if God wants to tell me something and I am not all there to listen to and obey Him?" And I will say to him: "My friend, do you think that you can block a divine or angelic thought from occurring? No one can do this. God can give you an idea to make you get up at this moment, to take the boat across Lake Lagoda and then off to St. Petersburg for a bowl of soup. And there's nothing you can do! After this, He can take you by the ear and put you on the train headed for Albania of all places. The next evening you might find yourself sleeping on a bench in Luxembourg."

Pilgrim) No one can put limits on God, we have to agree. So, what you are saying is that we limit demonic activity instead.

Monk) Most definitely. When we sit to pray with our nous in our heart, we have to know that any thought we have at this time is from the evil one. If God wants to communicate with us, He will do it without our knowing - we cannot stop Him. What we can do is descend with our attention down below our neck so the muddiness of evil thoughts will not rise. This is our objective during prayer, as the great ascetic St. Theophan the Recluse admonished his spiritual children: to have the nous - our concentrated focus - descend to the heart and there to be still before the Lord.

Please, could you tell us once again how we should enter into the haven of our chest to find undistractedness..

Monk) To have a good understanding of what the nous as attention is, you do this exercise: now, without the sense of touch, feel the left knee, then be attentive of your right elbow. Then, feel the back of your head, feel the right shoulder. Alright? The nous went wherever the sensation was. The nous can feel a body part without touching it and adheres to that spot, so we know if it hurts and is in need of healing...

Pilgrim) Ahh! I see. Very interesting. So, we can move it around our body using sensation.

Monk) Yes. Our nous which is the thoughts and our attention at the head, we control this nous, even though it is spirit, by physical means. The nous down in our heart uses the nous at the head to gather information and this nous is the attention needed to complete a task and to supply feedback to the nous at the heart, which is the control center, if you will, of our soul. Now, when the nous is solely up in our head the faculty of the imagination is very active and we cannot possibly curtail provocations, of all kinds. So we let this nous slide down through our breathing canal into our chest and we tuck it in there just like a baby in the cradle, as we gently breath out.

Pilgrim) Can we still think during prayer of the heart?

Monk) Yes, we do think, in fact more briskly, not swayed by our passions. But let us not forget that the brain in our head is a wonderful tool that our mind - our nous - uses to be able to act in living as a human being in this beautiful world. Well, let me see... this is what happens, when man is asleep his entire nous is found in his heart: his limbs, the body, the brain are resting. Now, as he awakes, a good chunk of the spirit in his heart which is the sovereign of his whole being and which is called nous escapes and pours out throughout the whole body, but mainly in the head to activate the brain. So, at this time there is nous in the heart and nous throughout all the flesh, they are of the same essence. And during noetic prayer the nous is gathered again, uniting at the heart so that distraction comes to an end.

Pilgrim) It unites when our feeling is concentrated in our chest near our physical our physical heart. Isn't that right?

Monk) Correct. It is like having a toothache. The nous, the attention that is, is there and that is all one thinks about. Still, there is something else to think of. There is another factor that

37

plays a pivotal role in this whole effort, along with our attention. And that is to glorify and to thank Him for what He bestows on us daily. We cannot forget this.

Pilgrim) How huge this is. Thank you, Father for reminding us that we should be thankful for everything. Unfortunately, we forget.

Monk) So there you have it: fasting, vigilance over your thoughts, fear of God, gratitude for all He does. And pray for me, the sinner. Watchfulness overall. Do not sadden the One who gave you life - have Him in mind at all times. If you do this you will see better days ahead. Go ahead now, I will see you in Church.

Pilgrim) Thank you again for your counsel and your words of encouragement...

Spiritual Tips

- *Strengthen your faith by having friends who themselves have faith.*
- *Have mercy on others. Compassion has greater value than any sacrifice.*
- *Do not remain idle. Idleness is the devil's workshop, and it is the forerunner to bouts of negligence of a spiritual nature.*

Hierodeacon) The Church, according to Saint Paul, is the mystery of communion of the Living Triune God with His children. The Church is also called the Body of our Lord Jesus Christ, or even His Kingdom on earth, but I, being a sinful man, understand the Church to be a hospital where man comes in to become healthy again.

Faithful) Is this why we go to Church? To find our health?

Hierodeacon) Initially, we as all people have to attend Church or to each their place of worship. All beliefs and religions have this innate desire, that everyone has in their hearts to know God and to love Him, as their driving force. But after coming to Church - we're speaking about Orthodoxy - the faithful have to be reminded, besides the tenets of our faith, the reason why we are here: that is to get well.

Faithful) So tell us: how are we ailing?

Hierodeacon) The same Saint, the great apostle Paul, knew of human weakness and so he explains in his epistle to the Romans, in chapter seven, that there is another law in our members. That is the law of the flesh which wars against the spirit. A conscientious Christian does not live in self-denial but understands he knows himself. And he knows God through his infirmities. He does not go to church to merely sit with the others, to hear a nice sermon.

Faithful) What does he do? What should we all do since we have the same nature?

Hierodeacon) Good. So, you understand that you are also in need of treatment. This is the first step one takes: to see all his faults, and to admit this and head to confession. Afterward he must try to refrain from committing the same infractions.

Faithful) Yet we succumb to temptation. What then?

Hierodeacon) You fall because you do not hate the sin. If you did, you would try harder. Temptations and passions are demons who want to take us down to hell. Do you want to flirt with them? Now, forgive me. Do not be so disheartened. Take it one day at a time as they say. Despairing over your troubles is not going to help. All I am saying is for you to try to passionately dislike the offer the evil one presents to you and to be prepared adequately beforehand.

Faithful) How do we prepare as you say?

Hierodeacon) By Nepsis. This word means watchfulness or vigilance. Watchfulness is unceasing attentiveness whereby a guard, if you will, is placed at the entrance to the mind to prevent uninvited thoughts from entering therein. The most sublime of all spiritual works is that of the guarding of one's mind to find stillness of thought.

Faithful) Is this more essential than prayer?

Hierodeacon) Prayer is part of Nepsis. No one can successfully keep a vigil on the senses, the heart, and the mind without employing some sort of prayer to do this. Of course, the Jesus prayer is the best prayer to use because it contains the name Jesus before which all knees shall bow according to apostle Peter. The Jesus prayer is awesome It is very powerful, and it is feared by the demons. When they hear it they freak out. With one "Lord Jesus Christ have mercy on me" they stir up a bit. After a second, they cluster, and by a third... gone!

Faithful) How is watchfulness accomplished? Do we just say the Jesus prayer?

Hierodeacon) I will tell you. Chronologically, those who want to please God, are aware of things appearing in their spiritual scope in the form of images and by the grace of God they distinguish good or evil in a matter of seconds. They quickly sweep the evil away consequently - but not by their own "muscle" And they know this. The way to perfection is to have this mechanism of one's soul, so to speak, become second nature. In the beginning it takes effort, sweat, and tears to stay vigilant but in time it becomes easy.

Faithful) Hmm. I want some of that. If you please.

Hierodeacon) Let me get the scoop (Smiles). Seriously though, you can acquire such a gift with not much effort... if you have a guide. It is easy if one knows how, and still easier if that person does not have many passions. Also, with a teacher a man can bypass all the troubles that his teacher went through to get to where he is currently. We see that in the life of St. Joseph the Hesychast as his disciples partook of this tremendous grace by simply doing obedience, grace which he acquired through untold toils, by an unbelievable amount of self-denial, and pain...

Faithful) Please do continue deacon M...

Hierodeacon) To start, one must find the time to pray. He must learn to pray attentively. To repeat saying the Jesus prayer orally over and over again and to adhere by his mind to the holy words of the prayer. At first, it will be hard to curtail the amount of thoughts and pictures coming in to disturb the peace, the conceptual images, insights and distractions. A barrage of seemingly innocent ideas will make their rounds to take charge of the cerebral haven up here at the head.

Faithful) I have experienced just that sometimes when I prayed.

Hierodeacon) You have to push through these clouds of distractions by repeating the prayer non-stop. "Lord Jesus Christ... Lord Jesus Christ..." When God sees that you are struggling for His love, He will give you what you want and need. The Lord exhorts us Himself in His gospel to knock and the door will open, to keep trying. After a while of oral prayer, the mouth sometimes gets sweetened and the heart also, from calling on the Divine Name.

Faithful) This is true. But now tell us how to take this prayer further. Thoughts assail us always.

Hierodeacon) The reason that your petitions may be dry is that you could be thinking as you are praying. Not that you can do anything about it, since only with God's help can the mind quiet down. This endeavor takes effort on our part but the Mighty One has to help stop the workings of the imagination. This faculty is the culprit. In order for thoughts to be made apparent in our spiritual viewfinder they have to take the form of a particular passion so to tempt us: I think that you do find some goodness and sweetness by praying but it turns sour as soon as pictures appear together with the thoughts and sinful conceptions. Am I correct?

Faithful) Definitely. Something small ruins the day, it doesn't take much.

Hierodeacon) Again, you have to cultivate a strong dislike even for little innocent-looking thoughts. You have to remember that not just evil thoughts are evil but good thoughts are evil and any other thought that comes during the time you are praying, all of them. None of them are any good. When Jesus came to walk on earth folks were possessed, lunatics, crazy, ill from numerous ailments. Our Lord demolished the works of the devils and put an end to them. Now they are like dogs without teeth. All they can do is give us thoughts. So, try that: Consider all thoughts during prayer evil in disguise.

Faithful) This makes sense.

Hierodeacon) I will show you how you can curb fantasy. This will also be of use. Matter of fact, if you can stop the imaginings, not just during Church services but at all other times as well, your prayer will become pure. The Holy fathers had the goal of a purified fantasy-free state of mind as their objective. All their lives they strove to preserve their spiritual vision unblemished. To start this work of purifying oneself, a man first learns how to use a prayer rope...

Faithful) Father, forgive me, this is how I pray at home. But please explain it to us.

Hierodeacon) Have you noticed that when you hold the rope in your hand, the thoughts you are assaulted by during prayer are much less? This is because your attention is split between the hand and head. For the imaginative faculty to work properly up at the head it needs all of our attention or focus, so if we focus on the prayer rope, it will not be able to produce so many images.

Faithful) I see. The evil one assaults us with images.

Hierodeacon) That's right. When man thinks of something straightaway he sees an image. And when he sees an image he starts to think. Therefore, if there is no image, no thought follows and there is no sin, and likewise when there is no thought there is no image and sin cannot follow. The mind needs that conceptual image to be provoked, otherwise it remains pure. And so, for the sinful image to strike, the mind's attention or focus, you could say, must be occupied with the sinful thought that this particular image represents.

Faithful) So we put the focus on Jesus?

Hierodeacon) Yes. While being attentive of the holy words pronounced "Lord Jesus Christ have mercy on me." And you turn the prayer rope in your hand to attract the rest of your focus to have the mind entirely absorbed in the prayer. This exercise promotes mental stability and with time a joyful feeling will appear to complement your effort and to bring you peace, and the rest of the gifts of the Spirit.

Faithful) Now, of all the other prayers, why the Jesus prayer?

Hierodeacon) Our Lord told us to ask in His name and we will receive. All the Orthodox Theology is contained in this single-phrased prayer. The other reason is that because it is short it helps us focus easier. Then there is the power in the Name and distractions cannot afford to stay around. The evil spirits are those distractions, and they get burned.

Faithful) Earlier you talked of the "Hospital" and our infirmities. What is the connection between these and the prayer to Jesus?

Hierodeacon) The mind, or what the Greeks define as Nous, is fragmented and ailing. I refer again to chapter seven of the epistle to the Romans. There we see that man cannot be what he wants to be because of his passions. Who can claim today that he is in control? One minute he's fine and then he starts to offend someone, or he will be raving incoherently at himself. For no apparent reason! And he can't do what he wants to do, he does not mean what he says being confused often times and then he is calm but envious of others, or gluttonous, lustful, greedy. The next minute he's praying in Church - Oh! He is as humble as one can be... With this prayer my friends, the Christian soul restores a balance and is reminded of God's presence, always.

Faithful) I call on Jesus, your reverence. And I feel more at peace and protected.

Hierodeacon) Sure. Now the reasons for unseemly behavior besides those caused by one's body's temperament and climatic conditions, come from the wiles of the dark spirits who find ways to intrude within our dimension to cause havoc, grief, dissension, quarrels, crimes, and misfortune. They have obtained rights since the fall of Adam, from mistakes committed by one's forefathers and down to the present times mainly because of our ignorance.

Faithful) So many mistakes. So many.

Hierodeacon) Part of it is because we cannot see the little rascals to know what they are up to. And then we do not pray the way we should. The way that I teach prayer has backbone; it is what I would call monk-friendly. I can't see the devils either but at times I feel them coming. Watchfulness has to kick in as I have mentioned to have any success in warding off the evils. Prayer for men of God is not just asking for this and that, like most people do as they sit in the pews cross-legged and waiting for the end of the service, but an earnest desire to cut down on their trespasses, and their afflictions and weaknesses.

Faithful) Of course there is confession and absolution. Right deacon? We can be forgiven.

Hierodeacon) God is so merciful. Yet, we should not rely so heavily on confession that we do not even make an effort to be on better ground the next time we see the priest. And certainly, just because we are present during all the Divine Liturgies, and we partake of Holy Communion does not miraculously change our status. We therefore have to prepare to receive the Holy Gifts. Preparation includes vigilance besides repentance and prayer.

Faithful) Can you tell us: what is the best time to pray?

Hierodeacon) Usually, early in the morning before going to work is the time when prayer is needed to get you out of your home on the right foot. You will cross yourself a few times while saying the Jesus prayer, then stand before your icon corner for a few seconds to give thanks to our Heavenly Father for everything he has bestowed upon you. After this you may find a dim spot to sit comfortably and to repeat the Jesus prayer for approximately ten to fifteen minutes with a sense of God's love.

Faithful) Is that all? I only get warmed up after about an hour or so.

Hierodeacon) Hmm... Look Isaak, we are not as holy as you are (smiles). Give the men here a break will you? But you too will have difficulties. So, sit and create an atmosphere before your icons. It is not easy to say the prayer undistractedly - in the very beginning a war begins. If you can get a minute in, I will give you my best prayer rope, a minute of stillness. I promise.

Faithful) Is it that hard to pray undistractedly?

Hierodeacon) It's impossible! Only with God's help can a man say, "Jesus." The evil ones will get stirred up once they get a whiff of the Jesus prayer. And they will try to put things in your head, many a thought. Like a hundred things you have to do, at that moment, when you are starting to pray. Right then. Still, in time it will get better and better yet. The mind will get accustomed to being gathered and focused and strong. This is how it becomes healthy - through adversity. It learns to push through, to neutralize our enemy's offensive, and to counterattack. The Holy Fathers say that nothing is stronger than the nous, the mind that is, when it is unified and wholesome.

Faithful) Tell us more about this unity, Father. I think we're onto something.

Hierodeacon) Once again, the nous/mind is fragmented. This is the illness of the human soul, and it is healed by obedience to the Church, by admitting that we are ill, as we have discussed, and by hating sin which the mind cultivates. The body brings to fruition absurd and senseless concepts until the mind comes to itself and puts an end to it. This mental gathering attracts Divine grace, which the demons abhor, and it puts to flight all evil distractions. So put the Jesus prayer to work for now and we will talk again. And pray for me the sinner.

Spiritual Tips

- *Adversity promotes mental and physical health.*
- *Depression comes from unfulfilled desires. Just be happy and grateful for what you do have.*
- *Do not trust any thoughts and do not believe in dreams. Reject, reject, reject... most thoughts are bad/negative thoughts.*
- *Before going to sleep, pin the icon of Panagia over your heart and read a few lines of the Akathist. "Rejoice, O bride unwedded." And thank God for everything once again.*
- *Sorrows and difficulties make us wiser.*
- *Read a bit of Holy Scripture every day.*
- *"Attach" the Jesus prayer close to the place of the heart and call on Jesus.*

Nick) Father, are you an Orthodox priest? Can I sit next to you?

Father) Yes, my child... You sound like an American, sit down. What are you doing in Tokyo of all places?

Nick) I work here. Bless me, Father... How about you? Do you work for the mission?

Father) I teach at the seminary.

Nick) Wonderful! Can you give me a word to go by, so that I can profit spiritually? I too am a student of Orthodox wisdom; I read the Fathers.

Father) Oh, are you? You do well to read. The Holy Fathers are the doctors who understand modern man. Even they who lived so far back in time but know of the anatomy of the soul and prescribe Spiritual medicine to heal it.

Nick) Could you tell me about this?

Father) Well, man is soul, body, and has grace as a conscience being the voice of God speaking and directing him toward His Kingdom. The body is flesh animated by the soul. And the soul has three powers: the nous, the logos and the spirit. These are the image of God in man.

Nick) Do they mirror, I think, God's three Hypostases?

Father) Faintly. But the nous, logos and spirit are only energies of the human soul unlike the Persons of the Holy Trinity, or Hypostases as they are called. Though, an analysis of these three energies does help us understand the relationship between the Father, the Son, and the Holy Spirit somewhat better...

Nick) I am listening, Father. Please continue.

Father) From your comment about the mirror I surmise that you have a good idea about theological matters in general.

Nick) My father was a deacon and his brother a priest, so I grew up in church and had the good fortune of mingling, since my youth, with men of letters; archpriests, bishops and teachers whose theoretical and practical knowledge was founded on a strong ecclesiastical foundation and tradition.

Father) I see... Now as the Father is nous and begets the Word, or Logos, Who is the wisdom of God, man's nous begets word and wisdom. And as the Holy Spirit is the Life-Giver, so man's spirit which issues from the nous gives life to his body. Does that sound right?

Nick) You know it... I tell you though: it gets confusing at times. And I wonder.

Father) No one knows who God is and we will never find out. As far as the function of our nous and logos, or what others call reason, there is an explanation why our actions make no sense. It is because we are ailing. If we come to terms with this truth, the world would be a better place. We also do not understand the saints and what they wrote because we are on another level.

Nick) We are also beguiled, I think, by the evil one and fall into error.

Father) That too. Do you wonder now why there is all this confusion?

Nick) What about the aspects of logic, desire, and anger that St. Maximus the Confessor refers to? What is your view?

Father) These pertain to the nous if I am not mistaken. Rational man has intelligence, and also desires, and has volition which manifests often as anger. This triad is subject to the passions, especially the desire and anger, and more often than not they are in disagreement as the interests of various virtues and/or vices clash during different occasions alone or in combination as they struggle to dominate over the nous.

49

Nick) In the mind there is chaos, therefore.

Father) Correct. Thus, the image of God in man is distorted. The three powers of the soul, the nous, logos and spirit, are out of kilter. The nous, or mind, is unstable because of the aforementioned and so the logos begotten of the nous is inconsistent, and the spirit which proceeds from the nous is unhealthy, transmitting illness to the body because of their union.

Nick) I know of the nous and the spirit but what really is the logos? You know, to have a better understanding of where it's to be found.

Father) In English it is termed the *discursive faculty*, but in Patristic literature it translates as the *inner word*. It is the voice of the heart with which we talk to ourselves mystically and read whole books without saying a single word with the mouth.

Nick) So when I say the Jesus prayer inside me...

Father) Your logos is saying it.

Nick) The monk who taught me how to pray with my heart told me to say the Jesus prayer in my chest among other things. But he didn't talk about the inner voice at all. He just said, "say the prayer inside you. " And this works for me.

Father) Sometimes the simple way is better. What profit will I gain from reading books if my heart is not there? Leave the terminology for people like me who talk a lot but who have no prayer. You do what your guide prescribed. Academics have no substance - the practical do the "talking" for they have experience and approach spiritual matters spiritually with faith and feeling. They are the true teachers.

Nick) Thank you, Father, for these nice words.

THE NOUS, PART 1

The nous is what makes a man very special. It is contained in the physical heart but not as in a vessel (St. Gregory Palamas) for it is spirit and cannot be contained. The nous is the "eye of the soul" and the image of God in us. It begets thoughts consciously in the heart as our Lord has disclosed to us (Matt 15:19). And nous is also the thoughts-logismoi which rise to the head to be analyzed and processed by our brain. This cerebral process and its by-products is known, in the modern usage, as Intellect. But the Intellect is not nous - the nous is found in the heart and rises to head level along with the thoughts. This "nous" that ascends to the head is called by the Holy Fathers "nous energy". This "nous energy" is produced, naturally, by the "nous essence" found in the heart as mentioned. Therefore, the nous divides into two parts: "essence" and "energy". The essence begets the thoughts and the energy rises...

Continued on page 98

Question) We appreciate you sitting here with us, Father... Please tell us about yourself and the work you are doing in this vast third-world country.

Answer) It is not easy to bring to mind my past, except that when I feel it profitable for an inquirer to know what I went through... and thus I speak from the heart on occasion about my troubled youth and God's love. I was born a pagan and therefore I had an excuse for being ignorant so the elder I found when I went to Cairo reproved me somewhat mildly and after some time baptized me. I made a vow never again to return to my home, fearing that I might lapse into thinking that I was then safe.

Q) How old were you when you left home? Did you not miss your parents?

A) I was almost thirteen years old, and I had just spent a whole summer in jail. My cell mate - a kindly old man named Owaku - introduced me to Christ and from then on I have not been the same. My parents, to whom I owe my existence, did not feel the same way about the faith I had only recently discovered and learned to love, but I stayed with them until Owaku was released, that same year. May God forgive them. A few weeks after, I bid them goodbye and with Owaku we embarked onto a caravan of merchants headed for Egypt. My old friend died there, and meanwhile I had found a job... it was in a Greek coffee shop, a stone's throw away from an Orthodox Church.

Q) And your spiritual father, your elder, who was he?

A) Father [...], a special person to whom I am greatly indebted. I worked in this shop for almost five years and attended every service in that nearby Church. Well... almost, I don't want to lie. After I was baptized I became my elder's acolyte and

52

closest companion – he treated me like his son. Later he took me along to Greece with his own family. We had bonded. So close in fact that I knew what he was thinking, and I was willing and ready at any moment to carry out his orders whatever they might insist upon. With his approval I was able to enroll in seminary. I served in the armed forces afterward, two years.

Q) Did you volunteer as a soldier? What was it like?

A) The two-year term is mandatory for all Greek male citizens and since by that time I had applied for and got the Citizenship, I had to serve. My mentor who saw ahead had made sure that I acquired an education. All along, I had cultivated my mother-tongue which was English; I went through gymnasium and the University of Athens, and I accepted this call with eagerness. The military was the best school. There, I did obedience, I learned how to live with others my age, and how to be orderly and clean. I also learned to be patient.

Q) Was the past behind you? How far had you come by then?

A) Well, I was incarcerated for petty theft several times in my youth - I was a member of a gang - but my folks did not seem to care. Then Owaku came into my life, and Christ my Lord who pacified my earthen heart making it light and airy. Then I understood that virtue was my only choice. Since that time, I cannot but walk the straight path. If I veer off this path, only slightly, my conscience disapproves and starts to censure me in a bad way - it gets violent. I cannot explain this to you. So, by the time I came out of the army, only remnants remained in my memory of my previous existence. But I tell you so as not to judge: now my belly is full! Hunger makes a man do things that he may come to regret, you know, bad things.

Q) How true is that? No one should condemn a thief.

A) The truth of it is, is that when we point fingers we lose the grace of God. If we come to the realization that there are people suffering, as we speak, then the world would be a better place. Because we would sympathize for one, and also we would be thankful that we are not sharing the same plight as our more unfortunate brothers out there - they could be us. Gratitude shown to our benefactor, God, for all the blessings He bestows on us daily can have a tremendous effect on our prayer life. As well as the feeling of empathy that I have mentioned. That helps also.

Q) So, is this a method for attracting divine grace? By feeling grateful?

A) Hmm. Now, let us not forget that a good Christian should not look for a method. He or she should love others, period. Let us call it something else then. We cannot be attracted toward this ideal for the reward end of it, but strictly for God's love. When we see our neighbor, we see God whom we love and obey. The holy Fathers who found prayer had great love for men, even for animals and for all of creation. And they submitted their will to another man, their Geronda, as for God Himself. Yet, this act drew divine grace by proportion of the quality of their obedience and so... by the feeling of gratefulness they were able to sustain the amount of grace bequeathed to each of them.

Q) You seem to be familiar with the relationship of the Geronda or Starets to his disciple. Could you tell us more about it?

A) In Cairo as a teen, I read a lot about the desert dwellers, their ascesis, the self-denial, and I practiced this self-emptying with my first elder of blessed memory. And with the presbytera even, and their son who was two years older than I. I also did obedience at work, in school, and of course in the army. That is how one finds peace of mind: to be submissive

- not a rebel - as our Lord was submissive to His Father. With obedience comes strength from above and wisdom. Whoever tries to live thus will never be disappointed...

Q) Could you please continue? This is very interesting.

A) After I came out of the army, I obtained a blessing from my adopted father and elder to join a monastery so that I could continue to live in this blissfulness that I was used to. You see, when I found the Lord I calmed down; when I listened and did as I was told I became better acquainted with prayer; and then with the gratitude that I spoke of I was able to seal - if you will - these gifts of calmness, peace, and prayer to have always since abiding in me. I found early enough that thankfulness must follow obedience. These two make a great pair.

Q) Did you become a monk there?

A) Yes, about twelve years later, before I was called to come and tend to my people, but in another region quite far from where I had originated. In doing missionary work in this continent monastic resilience, fortitude, patience are needed... and the constant memory of death. This work is no joke. The natives are in poverty and in need of care. And the obstacles are immense. Climates are hostile; distances between human habitations are great; transportation is almost non-existent, insufficient nevertheless; the terrain is treacherous.

Q) Why is that? Could you explain?

A) The landscape varies every few kilometers and no one knows what lurks on the way ahead. To slide into a gorge or into a lake, become trapped in quicksand, or walk through a meadow laced with poisonous crab grass is a common phenomenon. Every step one takes can be his last. And of course, the animals - big and small - I can't forget to mention the creatures living in these parts: the lions, crocodiles, hippopotamus, man-eating fish, snakes whose bodies are a foot in diameter. Not to speak of the ants which are the size of baby mice - they come out in the millions. These ants are unstoppable. They will devour herds of cattle. All these animals are a part of the terrain.

Q) How are you able to cope with such adversity?

A) I manage. Do not forget that I grew up in this environment, and as it is natural, I love my people. And I can identify with their hardship, their ways and living conditions. I have no problem sleeping on the ground hungry either. The natives here eat something every three days; they thank God for this. There are other countries where people starve. Like Ghana, where presumably a million children may be in danger of dying this year from hunger. I have to tell you that I also have prayer to console me at all times whether I am asleep or awake.

Q) Is this what the Apostle Paul wrote? Of the unceasing prayer?

A) Surely. It is possible for everyone to acquire unceasing prayer if they collect their mind. Frankly, this is very easy to do with some instruction and help from Above. Very easy. But who has time? In the "civilized" world that you boys come from, prayer is trivial. There are other things that men go for: the acquisition of wealth; education; a savory palate; jest and amusement; a mansion to live in, with maids. Let me see... a yacht, luxurious apparel. And if they cannot attain these goods, they will think and fantasize about them, when they sleep they'll dream that they are royalty, only to wake up as a pauper.

Q) We love to hear you say something on the topic of prayer, Father. But how do you know of our lives in the new world?

A) I have been there for a short time. There is opportunity for improvement - humanly speaking - in all aspects of living and that is very encouraging to see. But this great prosperity, apart from taking good care of the physical needs of the people, can sometimes be a hindrance to the acquisition of spiritual needs. The holy Fathers say that when the senses are satiated, the memory of God wanes....

Q) This is a fact. Forgive me. What precautions must we take to find a good balance?

A) Since plenitude is not evil, nor are fruitfulness and abundance, we must always thank God for all his gifts, from the air we breathe to the food we eat and for our home, for our for our family and our friends, for our work, etc. Because ungratefulness is evil. A human being must be taught, from a tot, to give thanks for all things. To really mean it, you know. Not for display as anything external, or required for the sake of some law, but for the gratitude to be an essential part of his soul sprouting forth when a favorable circumstance arises.

Q) Is this so important for prayer?

A) Yes, my good friends. Gratitude/thankfulness is the channel unceasing prayer flows out of, to irrigate the garden of one's heart to bring on consolation and joy. If prayer does not take this course, it would be like a body of water wasted on the weeds and thistles of life, instead of being guided out to the fields to cultivate the virtues, so to bring on the fruits of love, forgiveness and so forth. Well... you asked me to tell you something on prayer. This is how you too can collect your mind, by always giving thanks, as the same Apostle wrote in another epistle.

Q) Oh my. We have some thinking to do, don't we?

A) Let me simplify this concept to understand it better, for you have a way to go yet and can help others who you may travel among. You do what I do. See yourselves as a repentant man who have come home with a new lease on life. The parable of the prodigal son applies to all of us - you are not any better. And since our Father forgave us, and He forgives us, and He will continue to forgive us, and will keep loving us no matter what we do, then we have a good reason to appreciate Him and to also love Him. Do you see?

Q) That makes sense. But please... could you continue?

A) Of course. Now, by appreciating Him, you set the stage. Then the on-going theme of repentance keeps the fire of prayer lit. Thus, it flows effortlessly out of the heart. We appreciate and thank God ceaselessly even when we sleep, because sleep is also a great gift. You know how many people have trouble sleeping? To sleep, to walk, to eat, to be able to breathe: these are things we cannot take for granted. And by the way, this is the work I have done always as I try to instill gratitude into the minds of men, women and children. They do not have much but they appreciate what they do have. I make sure of that.

Q) What prayers go with this perfected mindset? Which do you suggest?

A) Prayers of a few words that one can easily memorize, to learn them by heart. But the fire of mindful prayer must be continually stoked by the memory of death, as I have mentioned. It goes back to being a missionary. The idea that one day our life on earth will come to an end, gives wings to a man. That, and the resilience afforded by a patient effort. All of these methods coupled with the constant invocation of those few prayerful words will bring bountiful results.

Q) Well thank you Father...we now have our work cut out for us. We will try our best to follow your instructions. Can you now please give us your priestly blessing? We forgot to receive it earlier.

A) Forgive me for I am not able. You have before you a simple monk who was never ordained. I am under obedience. I do some catechisms, I advise, and care for the livestock of our mission. I didn't mean to disappoint you. Have God's blessing, nevertheless.

Q) Oh no, Father. Please, do forgive us. It has been real... we think highly of you and are so glad that we have met.

A) I feel likewise. Go on now on the way of Peace.

Spiritual Tips

- *Patience is a great virtue.*
- *The man who does not take offense easily shows strength of character.*
- *Before opening your mouth, first control yourself, soothe your heart. Wait to speak until you are calm and composed.*
- *Try not to get too familiar with people.*
- *Do not judge hierarchs, priests, monks, or nuns. If you do, think of fire!*
- *Do not be obsessed with how you feel. Think of those who are naked, hungry, in jail, in hospitals, nursing homes, etc.*
- *As soon as you awake, cross yourself. Try to think about God before anything else.*
- *Do not begin your daily tasks without first having given a thought of gratitude to God for the new day, your health, all you have.*

Catechumen) Tell us father, after all we have learned about the Church, what about the mystical prayer, One-on-one with God, the prayer of the Saints. When will we advance to that other level?

Father) After your baptism into the Church which - God willing - will happen this coming year, you will be initiated in this most sublime work of the mind, that of noetic prayer, which can be called mental prayer or prayer of the mind, prayer of the heart or prayer of the nous.

Catechumen) Is this to do with the prayer to Jesus?

Father) Yes. The Jesus Prayer, "Lord Jesus Christ have mercy on me," is the rock on which the house of your faith is built, the strong unwavering conviction that God is present in our lives, in our thoughts, in all our actions. The Lord is watching and patiently waiting for us to call on Him for assistance.

Catechumen) This prayer has changed my life. Ever since you authorized us to say it orally, at the first session of our catechism, I have to confess that my thoughts aligned with the will of God, my attention in Church got better, and joy abounded.

Father) This is not a surprise. A swarm of evil thoughts assails the Christian who wants to engage in conversation with his Master. Before the advent of Christ on earth, people became ill, were possessed, moonstruck and walking the streets babbling incoherently. Jesus put an end to this. Before His Holy Name they were restored to bodily and mental health, tyrants were struck dead, the martyrs were strengthened, the dead were raised, sovereigns kneeled dressed in sackcloth, and the demons were rendered powerless.

Catechumen) Your words permeate my very being. Now, forgive me for I am simple, and I cannot so readily apprehend theological truths as the others in our group, I suppose. I have to confess though that, as I listen to your discourses, I am praying the way you have shown us and... my God, I can't explain it, maturity in the Christian faith is becoming for me a lived reality.

Father) God is impartial. He loves everyone the same. Orthodoxy is not about head knowledge, where knowing things intellectually makes a difference in one's relationship with Him. He does not look at secular power or possessions, either. Nothing attracts God more than simplicity of heart, like children have. So, approach - all of you - our God and Savior simply: "Lord Jesus Christ have mercy on me" without sophistries and clever ideas. Noetic prayer is like saying, "Whatever you want Lord, do with me, You know best."

Catechumen) I have come to the realization that our reasoning is being exploited by the evil one...

Father) This is exactly the case, forgive me for interrupting you. This is the problem, my friends. And that is why we have to keep our prayers short and plain without the "extras". Hey Benjamin, what are you doing there? You are always writing something. Talk to us.

Catechumen) This is good stuff, very interesting. So, you are saying that there's no need for small talk. I would guess that God knows everything. Just keep repeating the Lord's Name without asking for this and that. The Lord knows what we want... Let me make a note of this.

Father) In the Philokalia, St. Hesychios the Presbyter says that the mind of man is illumined to the degree that it is purged of impressions, concepts, thoughts, imaginings, etc. So, to know God in a personal way, one must clear the cerebral firmament,

61

as we had discussed at one point in the past and find some time to spend before our Creator. I have told you so, weeks ago, that we MUST find the quality time - this is crucial for our development - to be with the One we love, Christ Jesus without pretenses, fancy ideas, or mindful chatter.

Catechumen) I myself do this as you once suggested: I read from the prayer book before my icons. Then I stop and say the prayer to Jesus for a while until I get distracted, and then I back to the prayer book.

Father) There you go!

Catechumen) What about these distractions, Father? What can we do to stop them?

Father) If you are reading out of the prayer book, put your index finger under the line you are reading and move it along as you read. Or clearly pronounce the holy words aloud and try to listen carefully. If you want to pray with the Jesus Prayer, follow along intently as you repeat Christ's Name. If your attention escapes, bring it back and continue. If you keep doing this unfailingly, someday your mind will come of age to shuffle away any distractions coming your way, along with their byproducts, quickly and easily.

Catechumen) What do you mean by "byproducts"?

Father) Distractions are suggestions in disguise, and they carry passion more often than not. They are designed to take the focus away from prayer. Behind all of the distractions are the demons who cannot stand the Lord's Name to be recited. Notice how many thoughts spring out of nowhere as soon as you begin to pray?

Catechumen) You are right, teacher. Now please do explain this to us: what is happening in the spiritual plane that we must be aware of, so we can ward off these evils?

Father) These comments and questions you are raising have led me to believe that you have come a long way in your quest for knowledge. You see, when we started this catechesis eleven weeks ago, I had in mind that you should learn about the essential truths of the Orthodox faith by experience. You know, in a personal way, through prayer. And so, it seems that you do find quality time to be with God.

Catechumen) Let us not forget also that now we have the zeal. And so, we pray.

Father) Exactly! Now is the time to find out if what I teach you is real and not fake. And you will not "learn" intellectually. The mind of man - what the Greeks call "nous" - has the ability to taste the fruits of this academic theology we are now going over. And remember - we went over this point several times - the faculty of the imagination has to quiet down so that God will work to make Himself known in our hearts by contrition and a sense of love.

Catechumen) May I say something? When I cry sometimes my mind is so clear and it feels light as a feather. So, I guess contrition is a good thing.

Father) When sorrow over our sins reaches a certain level and tears of repentance flow out of our eyes, the grace of God consoles our soul and gives it wings. Then fantasy ceases to operate and the sweetness of prayer takes over. That is how one knows of things Divine. During such heartfelt moments God expresses the love He has for you and me and the whole world. Whereas before, uncertainty prevailed over matters of faith, now unquestioned confidence and trust in God has taken over.

Catechumen) Will our introduction into mental prayer after the Mystery of Baptism enhance this effort to find something higher?

Father) I promised that someday you will learn this prayer, but it seems - by the way you're going - that you may taste the fruits of this prayer before the fact. As I have once mentioned, this was my intention. I want you to experience the presence of God and the effect that it has on your heart.

Catechumen) You often speak of heart...

Father) Yes. The experience of His presence affects the heart of man positively: talk is cheap. That is because the mind is contained in one's heart, whose emotions and senses residing therein attest to the fact that God exists. Then the mind is also assured that God is real. Only when the heart comes to know God can the mind make the same conclusion rationally. If the mind does not have this conviction it falls into delusion and heresy because its theories and findings do not have the heart's stamp of approval. In other words, your intelligence, as students, must have proof that what I am teaching you is correct and genuine, and this proof is acquired by feeling through prayer.

Catechumen) What exactly do you mean by feeling?

Father) The heart feels - you all know this - and the brain reasons. The power of reason relies heavily on scientific evidence in order to operate decisively, but the heart's proof is in the pudding that the human mind comes to taste with the spoon of faith. Having faith initially helps us draw closer to God with the hope that He would give us a taste of the kingdom to come. If He does, an otherworldly feeling will envelop our very being. Then we will not only dismiss any doubts we may have concerning the mysteries of our faith, and also concerning the existence of God whom we cannot see, but we could - by the grace of God - enter into other spheres of knowledge unbeknownst to us up to that point.

Catechumen) I have a comment to make. I think that the Ten Commandments also play a key role in our progress. Is that right, Father?

Father) Precisely. We start there as we love our neighbor; we honor our parents... Afterwards, we find a quiet spot at home, and we create an atmosphere to pray and read God's word. But do forgive me... where were we in our Catechism? Ah! we were talking about the two natures of Christ. Let us continue...

Catechumen) One moment please, I also want to say something about prayer. Could I?

Father) Yes, Harlyn, go on.

Catechumen) Sometimes, when I least expect it, the Jesus Prayer is playing in my head on its own, and this brings me to tears. Well, I want to thank you, Father, that's all... I am grateful.

Spiritual Tips

- *Say a short prayer at intervals throughout the day to keep His memory alive.*
- *Sincerely greet everyone you meet in the morning.*
- *Do not give reign to idle curiosity. Through curiosity bad thoughts will come in to bother you later.*

SPIRITUAL AWARENESS TEST I

This theme might seem off topic but with these queries the nous (mind) is strengthened as it revolves around our faith even after our daily prayers and devotionals.

What was inside the Ark of the Covenant?
A portion of Manna, Aaron's Rod, and the Ten Commandments.

How old was Jesus when he began His ministry?
About thirty years of age.

Who is considered to be the first monk?
Saint Anthony the Great. He lived in the Egyptian desert.

Can a devout God-fearing Christian practice Yoga?
Certainly not. Yoga is an eastern religious practice.

What is the meaning of the word 'Christ'?
The Anointed One; The Messiah.

Name only Apostle who had a natural death.
Saint John the Theologian. He died around one hundred years old.

Who are 'the poor in spirit' of the Beatitudes?
Those who are totally dependent on God; the humble.

Which prophet anointed David a King?
The prophet Samuel.

How many did our Lord raise from the dead?
Three: Jairus's daughter, Widow's son, and Lazarus.

Which one of the twelve Apostles died in India?
The Apostle Thomas. He was killed there.

Where is Mount Athos located?
On a large peninsula in Northern Greece.

Who today are Ishmael's descendants?
The peoples of Arabia.

Do Christians believe in 'reincarnation'?
No. One time do we live on earth and then we die.

Which is the most popular devotional to the Theotokos?
The Akathist: the beauty and the grace of this wonderful hymn are unequaled.

Give two reasons why people go to Church.
An innate desire to know and to love God; a need to be protected from the evils.

What did Cyril and Methodius accomplish?
They evangelized and baptized the Slavs.

Which Pope of Rome wrote the Presanctified Liturgy?
Saint Gregory the Great (The Dialogist).

What is referred to as 'a window to Heaven'?
A Holy Icon.

Are the Angels immaterial in nature?
Only relatively. They have an ethereal body but not totally immaterial.

Is Patrick of Ireland a Saint of our Church?
Yes. He lived before the great Schism.

Name a well-known monastery in Palestine.
The monastery of St. Savas.

Is self-reliance a very great evil?
The snake imparted to the first man self-reliance and the thought that he can do without God.

Which great city was dedicated to Panagia?

Constantinople.

In what century was the Fourth Crusade?
The thirteenth century. They plundered
Constantinople and stole everything.

Why is the Jesus Prayer so powerful?
Before Jesus all knees shall bow.

Where was Saint John Damascene from?
The city of Damascus in Syria.

**Does memory of God weaken when senses
are satiated?**
That's for sure!

Why must one fight passions one at a time?
So, the man is not overwhelmed but
fights them slowly and steadily.

What is called the Great Commandment?
To love God with all one's mind, heart,
and strength.

Were there also another seventy apostles?
Yes, they also preached the gospel
throughout the world. Titus,
Barnabas...

**Tell us about Peter's first miracle, at the
temple.**
Peter said to the lame man: 'In the
name of Jesus of Nazareth get up and
walk!' And he did.

Who was the Centurion at the Lord's Crucifixion?
The martyr Saint Longinos.

What about the community in Lake Lagoda?
This historic monastery is called Valaam on an island in the largest European lake.

The sad story of Sampson, then and today:
Passions are destructive in every age.

What can we do for those who have reposed?
Memorial services, almsgiving, and private prayer.

What is the meaning of the word "firstborn"?
The first male child regardless of whether he is the only child; the heir.

The "feel good" of Orthodoxy - how to?
In attracting the grace of God by being righteous, prayerful, and temperate.

What is the mother of all of man's passions?
Self-love.

List some of the forms of ascesis.

Vigil, study, prayer, temperance, stillness.

How did Old Testament priests get answers from God?
They used unknown small items on the "ephod" to toss and decide yes or no.

Who discovered The Precious Cross in 326 A.D.?
Saint Helen, the mother of Constantine the Great, equal to the apostles.

Who wrote the life of Saint Anthony?
Saint Athanasios the Great.

What of the meekness of Jesus our Lord?
This is what man needs to inherit the earth.

Who are called "The Three Hierarchs?"
The saints: John Chrysostom, Basil the Great and Gregory the Theologian.

Against which passion do we fight first?
Gluttony.

Holy relics have performed countless miracles.
A dead man was raised when he came in contact with prophet Elisha's bones.

Amma Sarah lived by a river but never looked at it.
For the hermits of that era even looking out at the water was considered a sin.

How many kinds of tears can one have?
There are tears good and bad, from repentance, pride, joy, illness, love of God, egotism.

What are the three states of the nous?
Being in accordance with nature, contrary to nature, or above nature.

Was Israel the only monotheistic nation?
Yes. They were the chosen people.

The demoniacs confess that they are burned.
The prayer to Jesus does this.

How does a thought enter the heart?
Through one's spiritual vision.

Can someone in the world live the monastic ideal?
Of course. Considering that he simplifies his life.

For we saw His star arising... (Matthew 2:2)
"Anatolē" does not mean East when the article "te" precedes it.

Where is the Holy Trinity first mentioned?
In Genesis 1:26 - "Let us make man in Our image, according to Our likeness."

Will the coming antichrist be a real man?
So say the Fathers.

Can we see both physical and spiritual realities?
Yes, with our nous (the eye of the soul). And we can even feel these realities.

Who lived the longest of all men of the Bible?
Methuselah. He lived nine hundred and sixty-nine years.

Which men in the Old Testament saw Christ?
Adam, Abraham, Jacob, Moses, the youths in the furnace, Nebuchadnezzar.

Was Saint Gregory Palamas only a priest?
No. He was Archbishop of Thessalonica.

Did our Lord Jesus Christ ever laugh?
No, He did not.

For how long did Israelites wander in the desert?
For forty years.

How does spiritual delusion come about?
By believing in dreams, visions, signs, apparitions, prophesies, thoughts.

Where did the Holy Transfiguration take place?
On Mount Tabor.

How did St. Mary of Egypt cross the Jordan?
She walked on the water to meet St. Zosima on their second meeting.

How many nails held our Lord to the Cross?
There were four.

Which was the most renowned monastery of the Byzantine Empire?
The monastery of Studion in Constantinople.

How many came from Persia with the wise men?
It must have been a large caravan. Servants, animals for food, men of war for protection...

Can a serious Orthodox Christian meditate?
Never. Orthodox Christians pray.

The best and surest way to cleanse the heart?
Flee from the world.

THE DIALOGUES, PART 2

A DIALOGUE WITH A MONK ABOUT NOETIC PRAYER - SECOND TALK

Q) Thank you for the meal, Father. Just now I concentrated on the back of my shoulder and fantasy dispersed. Is this for real?

A) As real as the day is long. You know, in every field of human endeavor, such as in sports, in arts, or in music, we have the real professional, and the "wannabe". Pros who are genuine have their own style, form, techniques, and habits (and lots of secrets) related to their vocations. Monastics are not different: they have their own trade which cannot be taught by books and hearsay. They battle head-on with evil. Spiritual warfare is no joke and the battlefield of this warfare is the best teacher. A man does not attain wisdom just by reading some books. You know what they say? "If you are going to talk the talk, you have to walk the walk."

Q) I would like to ask: what is the chief reason we stumble in life?

A) Bad thoughts which are manifested as images up in the brain. We get assaulted by sensual fantasies. Not only by lustful sensuality, by the way, but by all the various earthly pleasures which please the senses. We "couple" with the enemy through our spiritual vision as we entertain these thoughts. We are deceived by illusions during the day and nocturnally by dreams. Bad thoughts, and the entertaining of them, feed our passions.

Q) So, the passions fight us. What then is this dispassion you had mentioned a while ago?

A) Dispassion is a cleansed heart freed from thoughts and passions, and from influences of the environment. Dispassion is sanctification of the powers of the soul, and eventually of the body also. Hesychasm and noetic prayer help to bring this about.

Q) I am confused by the word "dispassion;" does finding dispassion mean I should feel nothing?

A) Not at all. The "Philokalia" calls dispassion a state in which man exercises the passions "in accordance with their original purity and so without committing sin in act of thought." A dispassionate man may be impartial or detached from the passions and from sin but is not indifferent. "It consists, not in ceasing to feel the attacks of demons, but in no longer yielding to them. It is positive, not negative ... it is closely linked with the quality of love, and it is among the gifts of God."

Q) How does dispassion feel? How will we know if we have achieved it?

A) Do not expect to achieve any type of exalted spiritual state. Our goal is to clear our mind of all thoughts and distractions and, as my Geronda says, to "turn all aspects of our soul towards God." If we do this successfully, we will stop all spiritual attacks and distractions and open our hearts to God. Elder Ephriam says, "Dispassion does not signify a stoic indifference, but rather, a transfiguration and sanctification of the powers of the soul and eventually of the body also." It is normal for such prayer to feel "flat" or ineffective at first because we are not used to stopping all thoughts.

Q) As you are talking, I have been using the prayer rope. It truly helps. Could you comment on this?

A) As I said before, a monk uses the prayer rope to attract his nous to his hand, so that the thoughts and mental images will diminish. When you are turning a prayer rope your thought process will certainly suffer, as your nous is divided between

76

your head and hand. At the same time, this benefits our prayer to Jesus because thoughts, which we do not want while praying, are dismissed more easily as the fantasy subsides.

Q) What about prayer of the heart?

A) It's the same concept. Also, the idea I told you about feeling your hand with your nous is similar to the foregoing comment on the prayer rope. With all these methods, we are trying to clear our cerebral firmament of the clouds of fantasy. The devil uses fantasy as his main weapon, to disturb us, to give us anxiety and depression, to have us doubt the existence of God, to sin, and finally, God forbid, to throw us into Hell.

Q) About the nous: I am unable to fully understand this notion. Can you help me?

A) I will try. The nous is our think tank. It produces thoughts. It has consciousness and is aware and is "the eye of the soul." This title sheds light on the distinctive properties appropriate to its function. It has awareness, attention, and focus; the nous is all these three. By having these attributes, it can see, feel, and apprehend physical and spiritual realities. It can see and understand God to some extent, and it also has judgment. By the power of reason, it discerns, and decides...

Q) Please, can you continue?

A) In order to think, we need to be conscious of our thoughts or else they go unnoticed. Now, the nous is also called awareness as I've explained, or the attention, you could say. Our nous goes up and uses, the brain to process and analyze thoughts, like a computer guy. But see, the awareness, the guard who is also the custodian, has the keys to the office and it must be always there. If it happens to step out of the office for a minute, the thinking operation is disrupted, evil thoughts go unnoticed and prayer becomes pure.

Q) Hmm... So, we take this guy out of the office. "Who's on first"? (laughs)

A) Please allow me to veer off our path briefly to explain another factor which plays a key role in the acquisition of noetic or pure prayer. Your way of life must reflect your values. That is, you are called to be holy; set apart to God. Without this, you will never be able to train your volition adequately to gain control of your nous.

Q) Are there any other factors?

A) You are a knowledgeable bunch, professionals, academicians, and seminarians. So, a key factor is academic and secular knowledge. If you attempt to use secular knowledge and your reason to come to an understanding of God by virtue of noetic prayer, you are going to be disappointed. Rationalism is earthly. This tool will not work on prayer. It will be like using a chainsaw to slice a tomato: you are going to end up with tomato sauce. Prayer needs feeling, emotion, love for God, and... just enough brain.

Q) Is that all?

A) There is one more thing and that is simplicity. The three basic virtues in monasticism are: purity, poverty, and obedience. Poverty means shedding the extras, the extraneous elements of our lives. This virtue is not about being poor but being detached from all possessions, to not care about material possessions or things of the world. To break free from the shackles of matter and its byproducts and to live simply. This is a great achievement.

Q) Can't we own and enjoy things?

A) We are talking about freedom now, and the prayer. The heart of man can desire something to the point of obsession. Have you all noticed that, when you have a bad habit or an addiction you cannot control, you feel awful? This is true because we are made free, as our fore-parents were free in Paradise. This is the reason inner prayer cannot get off the ground – we allow too many "things" to encumber our souls. You must live simply for the heart to be free.

Q) Are we not free at this time?

4) Definitely not. You have to find happiness, my good friends, regardless of possessions, expensive clothing, and rich foods, modern technology, or conveniences. You are not truly free. Do you not believe me? Ok, let us consider a question: how many of you would like to be in Paradise at this time? Well? Raise your hands. Yes, in Paradise. In the Garden of Eden.

Q) I am in. Do you mean where Adam and Eve lived?

A) Yes, of course. I feel the excitement in the air, boy, oh boy! Oh, the smiles! Your approval gives me great joy. But now... brace yourselves. I assure you that you will not be able to live there for long. Do not let this surprise you. Paradise is not an amusement park. Bummer!

Q) What do you mean?

A) What I mean is that the Paradise in which Adam and Eve lived was a garden of fruit trees and other shrubs and greens with beautiful scenery, wildlife, waterfalls, etc. Really pretty. However, you will not sleep in a comfortable bed but under a tree on a bed of twigs and leaves, or in a burrow like the anchorites. There'd be no ice cream, burgers, or beer. No restaurants in the vicinity, no grocery stores, no clubs, nor gyms.

Q) Please, Father? You are killing me.

A) You want to go live in Paradise? With no TV or internet, no movies, video games, sports, or any other organized recreation? Not even a bike will you own, nor a car. The wheel had not yet been invented. There are no planes to fly places. No taxis nor buses. Not even a scooter. You have to go everywhere on foot.

Q) And why are you telling us all this?

A) Man cannot overindulge and then pray undistractedly. There would be always something missing and that something is poverty of spirit. To need only the essentials, this is the key to prayer and also to happiness.

Q) Is happiness a result of prayer, or is prayer a result of happiness?

A) This question, believe it or not, fuels the fundamental reason of why we pray and go to church. Those outside of the Church are miserable; that's a fact. Happiness then is a result of prayer, but true prayer is also a result of happiness. When we pray with joy, we pray well and are fulfilled; however, when we are not happy, and pray without joy, usually we fall into negligence.

Q) What is the connection between over-indulgence and negligence, if any?

A) There is a cycle of over-indulgence, addiction, unhappiness, and negligence. When we overindulge, we become habitually dependent. Then we are unhappy because we cannot stop this addiction, and negligence comes over to top it off. Then, seeing ourselves being negligent as regards to our prayer life, we fall into overindulgence to find some joy. And then again, we are unhappy with ourselves mainly because of conscious pangs for the addiction are getting out of hand and our negligence flairs up. God is not happy, His grace withdraws, and we keep over-indulging...

Q) And? What is there to do?

A) Once again, we'll be ok as long as we are not "attached". In his vault in the palace, Emperor Justinian had a heap of gold. That did not prevent him from being a Saint. "Live simply," is all I am saying. The secret of prayer is not to have many desires. To be content with what the Lord gives. And if you want to excel spiritually and ascend to other levels, be happy with nothing.

Q) Your words are profound. Is this how we find prayer then?

A) The stage is set. First, be simple, humble that is. Humility brings tears. "A humble and contrite heart, God will not despise" (Psalm 50). Second, love and honor the ones who brought you to life and raised you: your parents. Third, have a priest by your side to reveal your thoughts to him before falling into sin.

Q) As a means of prevention?

A) You got it. After a man meets these first three criteria, the fourth step is to start repeating the Jesus Prayer. Start speaking the prayer while being attentive to the holy words pronounced and pray this with a feeling of love for the Lord. The fifth step is to take turns saying the prayer sometimes with the mouth and sometimes inaudibly with the inner voice. Meanwhile, it is proper and helpful to turn the knots on a prayer rope during both the fourth and fifth step.

Q) Father, what about book prayers, where do they fit in?

A) Book prayers said orally are straight prayer. We examined straight prayer briefly in the very beginning of our talks. With book prayers, it is talking to God using someone else's intellectual creations. Book prayers have much value, as do improvised prayers coming from our heart. But when we pray this way the faculty of our imagination is active, and we cannot escape distraction. St. Gregory of Sinai says that expending our energy in reciting psalms makes the intellect grow slack and ruins our ability to pray firmly and resolutely.

Q) But how are we going to ask God for things?

A) God knows what we want. Intellectual meditation, reflection, stipulation as by planning to coerce the will of God to serve our purpose, will not work to bring on Divine grace. On the contrary, where our spiritual doors are open to the suggestion of the evil spirits, we are easily deceived. People erroneously think that they will draw God's attention by using many words. Further, placing more effort on recitation of written prayer and less on inner prayer is a lower, and less effective, state of prayer, according to St Gregory because it means "abandoning the interior presence of God" and addressing "yourself to Him from without."

Q) Is this how we fall prey to these evil things?

A) Surely. The imagination is the bridge of the demons. When we make up words to talk to God, we are thinking, we are, therefore, imagining. And this imagination is how they come in, if we are not careful or knowledgeable.

Q) Does it matter what language we use to say the Jesus Prayer?

A) Do not worry about that. Talk to the Lord in your own language. He wants you to love Him, that's all. If you happen to be in some Church and you do not understand the words uttered by the priest keep in mind that your soul understands. This is another fault some have: they have a need to hear and understand every word of the service or liturgy. Some even pressure their pastors to say the prayers which are supposed to be said mystically out loud so the congregation can hear, as if that were going to matter. If it were imperative to understand the language to receive grace, why would we bring kids and babies to Church?

Q) What are you trying to say by this?

A) Actually, what I had in mind is, to use the language question you brought into view, to have the mystery of noetic prayer solved. Can you recognize the fact that God illumines all peoples without their knowing? Do you see? Straight prayer relies on intellectual activity while circular/noetic prayer tunes it down to a minimum; God is in our hearts and understanding us without words. And God still gives us His grace.

Q) We get it. Please do continue.

A) When we pray, there is no need to ask for this or that. St. Hesychios the Presbyter says that God illumines the nous always but more so when it is purged of all concepts, thoughts, ideas, images, fantasies. This is huge. Put away all intellectual products, except, "Lord Jesus Christ have mercy on me." Do not think about things. Do not daydream or imagine anything and, within weeks, if you pray this way, your nous will strengthen.

Q) Can you tell us the sixth step?

A) The sixth step, and the rest which follow, depend on your comprehension of the term "nous." The nous makes thoughts, and it also has consciousness. Man is aware unlike the trees, and unlike other animate species, he has awareness of God...

Q) And?

A) And the nous, which is spirit, exists inside the bodily heart. It's an immaterial substance – no one knows what it's made of. Now, the nous begets thoughts which are then sent up to the brain, to be analyzed and processed. This process is made possible by our consciousness which the nous uses so to be aware of all things in the spiritual and physical planes. This consciousness or awareness the fathers also define as nous.

Q) We need to strengthen the nous?

A) Correct. Don't forget that the nous has three powers: desire, intelligence, and volition (willpower). When we desire something that is evil, the fantasy up at our head dresses the desire with an image to scrutinize it properly, but our intelligence examines it and disapproves. Then, with the help of our volition, the intelligence chases the desire away before it takes root. The nous is the guard and uses these three powers, which need to be strengthened and trained to be always on guard. We can strengthen the aspect of desire by fasting, the volition by long-suffering (patience) and doing good works, and the intelligence through praying and reading scripture.

Q) How do the intelligence and willpower chase evil desires away?

A) By the power and help of the Almighty. Yet they also have to be healthy and strong. And these aspects or powers of the nous become healthy through hardships and patience, as we have already discussed. If we cannot ward off a provocative thought right off the bat, then we go to plan B, which is to be inattentive of the thought's conceptual image and both thought and image will vanish.

Q) And how do we do this, again?

A) Listen carefully. Our nous, as we have discussed, is also defined as awareness, and this includes awareness of our entire body. When we have a toothache, our nous is now there on the tooth – the tooth has our attention and focus. When our knee hurts, there goes the nous to the pain. Where we have feeling or sensation, our nous (our attention) goes. When our nous is at the head, we are able to think. But, when we take our nous (the attention) from there and put it on the prayer rope, our thought process is disturbed, and images cannot readily be created by the imagination.

Q) So, we can put the nous in the heart, at will? And how?

A) We do this in several ways. But I have to say: this is not trigonometry; it is easy. And there is nothing mysterious or strange, like your mind would have you believe. Look, take the index finger of your right hand and press on your chest at the place of the heart. You got it? Just like that. Now, take your hand away. Do you feel that spot?

Q) I feel it. And now?

A) Keep your feeling right on that spot. Notice a difference? If you continue to focus there, the fantasy will start to go out-of-whack and the thoughts will be less. You will finally be in control, and little by little your mind will gain momentum to be able to dismiss the evil coming its way. To alleviate distraction, pray while you have your nous on your heart, on your hand, as I have mentioned, or even on your stomach. Do you remember what I have told you about breathing with the Jesus Prayer? Well, all these things are very useful. They help establish inner prayer. At one point, your heart will begin to say the prayer on its own.

Q) I am still breathing in the Jesus Prayer, Father, as you taught us. Do you think that it might continue?

A) In Luke 11:9 the Lord tells us: ""Ask and It shall be given to you. Seek and you will find." This is Orthodoxy and if someone wants a gift, he will get it. To maintain the prayer, ask the Lord. Our faith has miraculous stories about the martyrs defying the emperors, about great miracles, dragon slayers, saints who did not eat for forty years. Others did not give their eyelids rest or slept in a lion's den and inside the graves. So, if you want something, believe and it will come to pass.

Q) But the thoughts say otherwise, what are we to do?

A) Nothing. Let them be. Have your goal before you. Do not let matter rule over your spirit and the outcome of that struggle will pay off big dividends. Shoot for Paradise without attachments, addictions, or bad habits. And tell me, do you have to sit in front of that screen for hours on end?

Q) Father, you forbid us to have our phones here: when I leave, I will feel cleaner for three days. How is that?

A) You all know that today's electronics promote immorality. Besides this, it also destroys intellect and drives ADHD. Those who pray cannot control their mind because of attention deficit. The right formula for any Churchgoer is to live like God intended for him to live, in the Garden of Eden. When you have your child play in the dirt with mom while you plant a field of vegetables, or as you go and break a sweat cutting firewood for winter, then you know that a feeling of well-being is about to arrive. You are now in "accordance to nature" mode, and so is your family. Modern electronics have introduced a major distraction from living our lives as intended by God; one which is not only hugely time-consuming but also injects every conceivable form of immorality directly into our minds.

Q) I want to ask something. You mentioned intellect. What is that?

A) The nous or mind ascends to the head and, once there, reasons using the logical faculties of conscious thinking and cogitation. It formulates ideas and concepts from information that it brings up from the heart. I guess you can say that the nous becomes intellect when it reaches the haven of one's brain.

Q) Why not use intellect as an appropriate definition for nous?

A) Because the nous is located in our heart. The intellect is arranged logically at the head. So, the intellect does not have the requirements to act like a nous, which is all eyes, conscious, aware of itself and its mission, and which acts as reins for unrestrained brainstorming, as it often happens.

Furthermore, without the awareness which the nous provides, the intellect goes up in smoke. It disappears, as if it had never existed.

Q) Is that why monastics shift their attention?

A) Bravo you. This is prayer of the heart. The nous comes up to the head. Then, it uses the brain to express itself and to evaluate its thoughts which manifest there as images. The experienced monk makes the nous take a U-turn by putting his attention/focus on his heart whence the nous came. So, the nous returns back to the heart. As a result, the brain goes blank.

Q) Is that why they call it pure prayer?

A) Yes. Its purity is the undistractedness afforded to those who pray this way. Now people, throughout our talks I have been repeating myself. It is like when I prepare to make bread, and well, I keep kneading the dough of prayer to have a better rise.

Q) It's all good. Please, knead some more.

A) When you sit to pray One-on-one with the Lord, make sure that you are 100% alert. This is very important. When the brain and nous are shutting down, imagination begins.

Q) What do we expect to feel during noetic prayer?

A) Nothing by way of the senses. A little emotion, love for God and all peoples, repentance, and peace; these are good things one feels during prayer. The old-timers back home were wholesome. They weren't exposed to what we see around us today. And they did not look for signs, visions, sensual feelings, comfort, ecstasy when they prayed. They were overcome by feelings of love and gratitude that He rained upon their crops and gave them shelter and a family to look after.

Q) What do you mean by "what we see around us today"?

A) The forces of darkness have broken through man's defenses. Demonic possession is most prevalent today among our youth, our hope for tomorrow. It is getting worse and worse. God help us.

Q) Can ecstasy or theoria be achieved today as we read in ascetical literature?

A) Theoria is for monks only. Purity of body and soul must proceed before entering into this stage. My elder admitted that he had ecstatic prayer. But it is not for the laity to enter this realm, nor to behold God. Fortunately, most people understand, except for a few who live in another world. So yes, noetic prayer is for mostly everyone but theoria is not.

Q). So, any fears are unfounded?

A) Absolutely. In my youth I was also deceived to think that *prelest* was an issue in regard to mystical prayers. Many millions of Christians have prayed noetically throughout thousands of years. And of course, the Hebrew patriarchs, Moses, Elijah, the All-holy Theotokos, the apostles, the saints, martyrs, all monks and nuns, and laymen.

Q) Why is there ignorance in world Orthodoxy today?

A) Because the devil wants us to stay in grade school. Let no one speak in haste concerning Divine things, lest he fall into a grave error. St. Ephraim of Katounakia has disclosed to us that preschoolers will not know of high school until they get there. You Should have seen my grandmom praying with such fervor. She'd put us to shame. She was in "college."

Q) And you say this is what we need?

A) Noetic prayer. We have the Name of the Lord, "Lord Jesus Christ, have mercy on me." In time it will go inside of a man to call on Jesus at all times, during any occupation or pastime. I tell you, with confidence in our brotherhood's tradition, that a pure lifestyle, coupled with revelation of thoughts and the

Jesus Prayer, is more than enough to bring on stillness and peace of mind.

Q) What about Holy Communion?

A) That goes without saying. I tell you boys: even though you know the answer to most questions that you raise, you are humble enough to sit here and listen to an old man. You have read tons of books.

Q) We know nothing, Father, could you tell us of other techniques to return the nous to the heart?

A) Alright. St. Kallistos, Patriarch of Constantinople, says that God the Father poured into our bodily hearts His breath or, as St. Kallistos called it, "noetic sensation." Noetic means pertaining to the nous, this sensation allows us to feel the place where our nous is located. So, we can move the nous at will by feeling. When we feel our knee, the nous is there.

Q) So, our mind can feel?

A) Our mind, or nous, produces thoughts non-stop, this is one of its functions. It also has awareness by which it moves about. When we have a mosquito on our arm, for example, the nous feels it and "gives us a holler" to chase it away. The nous can also see.

Q) How is the nous able to see?

A) The nous can see by the sense of touch. You know, when you are in a dark room, you can feel your way around by touching the walls, the furniture, etc. Further, you can perceive with your mind's eye where you are and what the chairs and table and things look like. Or when you feel an item with your hands while your eyes are shut, you can "see" what this item looks like by feeling it.

Q) Could you tell us about the breathing technique used to find the heart?

A) Do you understand what you are trying to accomplish by prayer? By any prayer? Do you realize that noetic prayer is not a means of bringing on enjoyment and excitement, but a feeling of love for God and neighbor, and a way to find undistractedness and focus? How can Divine grace act to soothe and heal an aching heart when a man is looking for a good time, or for visions and things like out-of-body experiences, lights and revelations? If one is looking for rapture and spiritual awakening so as to revel and "feel" the spirit, so to speak, and to acquire metaphysical knowledge, he will not achieve pure prayer. Are you ready to put away these thoughts that might creep in while praying?

Q) Yes, I believe that I am ready. Then what?

A) Then seek the "dispassion" we spoke of earlier. Start by not accepting any sort of a good feeling, while praying, or any speculation, and dismissing all phenomenon. Reject not just prideful thoughts but ALL thoughts, even if they seem to be salvific and holy. And when you finally realize that only God gives prayer after closing the doors of the soul to fantasy, then prepare yourself for mystical One-on-one prayer with the Lord via the invocation of His Name. And be humble; that is, accept the fact that you are cheap, as we all are.

Q) What if we cannot handle this kind of self-reproach?

A) If you have an inferiority complex, you will not be able to pray, because this is pride in disguise. Feeling superior is the flip side of this same coin. Now, if you understand how to move the nous about, what the nous is, and you keep in mind that the fantasies and distractions must be rejected, the next phase entails picking up the prayer with the breath, as I have already taught you.

Q) You mean to breathe in the Prayer?

A) Yes. We pull the Jesus Prayer, "Lord Jesus Christ...", with the breath into the lung area and stop momentarily. Where our breath stops, this is the heart. Our nous (our focus) has come into this hollow through the air canal along with the words of the Prayer. As soon as the nous comes into our chest and snuggles against our lungs and our physical heart, it becomes aware of its surroundings. It will then find, by feeling/sensation, a spot to which to attach.

Q) So, it can feel without touching?

A) Our nous has sensation. It can corporeally discern on its own, without employing the sense of touch for that purpose. We guide it down inside our chest, like something solid, and it gathers information to send it directly to our brain for screening.

Q) And we guide it down by inhalation?

A) Exactly! And when we breathe out saying the Jesus Prayer, the nous stays in the chest, it does not come out with the air; we trap it. It stays down under permanently following the prayer as we inhale and exhale. The concept is really easy to understand. The nous is this noetic sensation that we feel inside our chest. As long as it stays put, close to or over our bodily heart, the faculty of the imagination cannot function. Thus, our prayer becomes pure, our soul is enlightened by God. His rays penetrate our very being as they cleanse our heart gradually of all iniquity.

Q) This is easy. I have read a lot on this subject. Why couldn't I come up with a good explanation?

A) This question is often asked. I would think that sometimes the Lord hides good things behind veils of mystery. I guess He has His own reasons. As simple as it is, it is so much harder for some people to grasp.

91

Q) You could've told us everything earlier. Why did you give us the runaround?

A) Did not Jesus say that God the Father has hidden Divine truths from the wise and prudent and has revealed them to babes? Is this not the reason that smart people go on the warpath concerning noetic prayer? Because they are baffled, looking for deep meanings in complicated learning, rather than following God with purity and simplicity? And I say to you: Help yourselves, find a father-confessor first, recite the Jesus prayer as the anonymous author of The Way of the Pilgrim did, and read the Philokalia, The Art of Prayer, and Counsels from the Holy Mountain, and do not think highly of your own intelligence. Take it slow and be consistent.

Q) You mean to take baby steps?

A) Exactly. Along with oral prayer let the passions come down a bit, have patience during temptations, know that self-reliance is evil, as we have pointed out, and seek out your spiritual guide/confessor as needed. And carry a prayer rope in Church, say the prayer under your breath so as not to irritate others around you. Honor your parents, love thy neighbor, obey your conscience, remain pure to the best of your ability, and do not let sins fester unconfessed. When you have a little time and you are totally alert, breathe in the prayer and then out with your bellows, the lungs, as they pull and push the air along with the holy words gently in and out of your chest.

Q) I have been doing this for years. Why do I get a pain sometimes, here on my heart?

A) Well, to explain this occurrence: it plays a most important role in the gathering of our attention. When we abandon the natural rhythm of breathing as we inhale and exhale slowly, less oxygen goes to the heart. This creates a slight harmless pain there, attracting the nous like a magnet.

Q) I also have this. But it turns into a good feeling. Does this bring about the union of heart and nous?

A) It does. This little pinch at the heart serves as the butler - have no worries - a spiritual feast is about to begin. Now, there is not a pain in my heart; some people do not get one. But if you ever do, remember my words and you will not be disappointed. God has withheld such things for His children, His babes.

Q) The butler, huh?

A) My butler is a little tug at the heart and, sometimes, tears. Others rely on a state of repentance to get going, and yet others warm up their heart for prayer with the remembrance of death. The time spent with the prayer of the heart can be a source of spiritual sweetness and joy for all these cases, and for all peoples. Glory be to God for all things!

Q) How do we know if the spiritual sweetness and joy are real and not fake?

A) Did we go over this? The safety for an Orthodox Christian, my friends, is to reveal to our priest everything. Whether it's a vision, a dream, gladness, warmth of heart, or anything else. If it is not something good, when we reveal it, it does not come to bother us again. There is "demonic energy" caused by dark spirits, and "divine energy". The demonic joy is counterfeit, having a rush, hype, excitement, carnal arousal, agitation, and loss of breath as its attributes. The Divine is love, contentment, fulfillment, calm and peace – something you will certainly not find on TV or the computer. For the modern, carnal man, the divine energy seems boring.

Q) Is that why when I go on, I can't get up off my seat?

A) Demonic joy gets on you like a leech, and it will delete any good deed you have accomplished that day. It will not let you get up to go to sleep early enough to be able to pray the next day. And you think that by sitting there you will be made holier? Keep watching. That screen will wrap around your mind.

Q) This is me, is there any hope left, you think?

A) I see this trend now, the light at the end of the tunnel. Our youth are fed up with the usual. Kids are smart today, they have heard every sermon and side-story and are looking for something more, the practical and the mystical. A human wants to reach out to his maker, to communicate, to love Him.

Q) Please Father, could you tell us once again why the nous must return to the heart?

A) When the heart, the nous, and the will (the three powers of the soul) come together, man unites with God. Beside this, God resides in man's spiritual heart which is situated inside his physical heart. We cannot feel or see spiritually but we do come in contact with the physical heart by way of sensation, and by extension we make contact with the spiritual heart. Thus, having the nous close to his heart, a man can apprehend divine things by the emotions and feelings in his physical heart.

Q) Say it again?

A) Our hearts are like radios picking up signals from the demons and angels. St. Paisios of the Holy Mountain urged us to turn the dial to the right frequency. Although the physical heart is flesh, it is affected by the spiritual heart by virtue of the union of the physical and spiritual and acts accordingly. When we are happy, the heart beats happily and smoothly. When we are angry, it beats unevenly and quickly, and so forth.

Q) And the Jesus Prayer? Where exactly does it come into play?

A) If you followed what I have said, you will have noticed that there is a particular location in our body from which evil thoughts spring out. This location is right above our physical heart. The faculty which transmits to us all thoughts, conceptual images, and ideas from the spiritual world, to be analyzed by our reason is there at the top of the heart. It is called *logos*; this is our inner voice.

Q) Isn't this interesting?

A) When taken up by a demon, the inner voice spits blasphemies, plays hard rock, creates obscene scenarios, etc. When an angel takes control of the inner voice a man hears Byzantine chant, has good thoughts, creates disposition of good will for all mankind. Therefore, a monk or anyone interested in acquiring holiness must turn the dial to God's channel, and he or she does this by taking over this faculty and giving it godly things, words, and concepts to think about and to utter.

Q) Unbelievable! So, our inner voice is up for grabs?

A) That's right. The inner voice is what the devil and a man of God fight over. This fight is continuous, it never ends. This voice is the voice of the heart by which we talk to ourselves, write essays, and read whole books mystically. By this voice we also sin and come to imagine terrible things; God help us!

Q) Why is this voice on the loose?

A) Because we are free and rational beings. And our Lord wants us to freely choose Him as our master. So, our nous, this vagabond who roams the streets and alleys must go back to tidy up his home. He descends into the cavern of the chest, finds and seizes the inner voice, by force if he has to, and gives it God's Holy Name to pronounce and to think about.

Q) If the nous can seize the inner voice, why do we struggle?

A) Because we often are actively distracting the nous from this work and even working against our own interests. If we start the work of cleaning out the temple of the Holy Spirit, which is our body/heart, through prayer and, yet simultaneously continue to pour sinful images, media, thoughts, memories, and ideas into the temple, we will never become clean. We must help ourselves achieve prayer and communion with God through simplicity and purity.

Q) And then?

A) Then, in time, the heart comes into stillness; what the neptic fathers call *hesychia*, quietude. When there is no loud music playing in the mind, no sinful spectacles or tendencies to tame, Christ has been enthroned within.

Q) Can you give us an idea what that feels like?

A) The word to describe this state of mind is blissfulness. But it is not the "blissfulness" a carnal man is used to, with strange dreams, apparitions, sexual appetites, new-age mysticism, daydreams, sensual excitement, astral journeys, substance abuse, and the highs of acquisition of wealth and of power. This awesome feeling of divine blissfulness comes from dispassion, not having any desires but for the love of God and detachment from matter.

Q) As you were saying earlier, this is Paradise?

A) Correct. A man who loves God and his fellow man, and does not care for things, lives his Paradise from this life. Isn't that what our Lord Jesus Christ taught us? What did he say: "Take my yoke upon you and learn from me, for I am gentle and lowly in heart, and you will find rest for your souls". Our Savior and Teacher had no desires except for our salvation. He walked the earth He built, barefoot, and had no home or possessions. He even gave up His life.

Q) So, dispassion is a great feat?

A) Dispassion is Holiness and the prayer helps to bring it on. My elder told us that only noetic prayer can work the heart to give us dispassion and freedom. In the first centuries of Christianity, those Christians and monks who attained perfection did it with hardship, fasting, prostrations, sleeping

96

on the ground or standing, temperance and abstinence to a great degree. Today we have this prayer to get the same results. But let us continue later, I just remembered the wax tank is on. Come with me, if you like, and we will dip a few hundred candles and continue our talk afterwards.

Continued on page 160

Spiritual Tips

- *The Orthodox do not pray with imagination.*
- *Fantasy is the bridge of the demons.*
- *The faculty of the imagination "dresses" every thought with a correlating picture.*
- *Thoughts then come up to the head and manifest as images.*
- *The devil tries to arouse the fantasy to start trouble.*
- *Noetic prayer is prayer of the nous.*
- *With prayer the nous quiets down. This is called "stillness" or "hesychia."*
- *The objective of noetic prayer is to stop the workings of the imaginative faculty.*
- *To pray undistractedly by subtracting the focus/attention from the head.*

97

THE NOUS, PART 2

...to use the brain to analyze, and to solve, to figure-out and to reason. This process, again, is the work of the Intellect which reasons erroneously, more often than not, because of passion. Meanwhile down below at the heart-level battles are won and lost. The "nous essence" residing there, is assaulted constantly by this or that evil thought and it usually succumbs to desire. This happens because the "nous energy" is occupied at the head with different concepts and so the nous is divided-fragmented. In order to fight the evils that come in successfully, the "nous energy" must descend to the heart to unite with the "nous essence". And then there will be unity in thought, desire, and action. "But how will this occur?" Ask the uninitiated. "Will we have to bring our brain down to the heart?" Perplexed as they are they obstruct those who want to come closer to Christ. "No, my child, it is not for you." they exclaim with...

Continued on page 159

Hesychast) Welcome to my hut. Rest from the noise and the worldly confusion. You too, my son, sit with the others - are all four of you together?

Pilgrim) Yes father, we have come to see you. Tell us please, something about prayer.

Hesychast) Well prayer is how the little man communicates with God, and so there are three kinds: the straight prayer, the spiral and the circular. The straight and the spiral are those improvised prayers with or without the use of spiritual meditation, and there is circular or "pure" prayer.

Pilgrim) We are aware of the first two and we would like to know about the third, which is why we came.

Hesychast) The third one is the renowned "noetic prayer" or prayer of the heart, when the mind leaves the externals, goes inside a person and latches onto the remembrance of God through a continuous invocation of the prayer: "Lord Jesus Christ have mercy on me."

Pilgrim) And... could everyone achieve this gathering of the mind to be able to pray well?

Hesychast) The mind, or what the Holy Fathers call "nous," is fragmented today. This is the illness of the age. Back in the day, folks lived simply, and they were mentally sharp. So, noetic prayer is innate in everyone, but those who excel in it are very few, mainly because of electronics. A short attention span allows the nous to wander.

Pilgrim) I guess being "all there" helps a lot in this endeavor.

Hesychast) In regard to circular prayer, attentiveness is the key. Otherwise, purity of thought cannot be achieved. We collect our nous to stop the fantasy and the fanfare of the passions.

But to do this, a certain technique is used and by this way and the grace of God, a man will finally acquire a good state of mind if he is humble enough to follow instructions, of course.

Pilgrim) Can you tell us about this, Father? We will faithfully follow your guidance.

Hesychast) Our objective is to put a halt to the evil coming out of our heart, we therefore let our nous descend to the chest level, and we pray there. When attention is fixed on the place of the heart, control over various thoughts comes easier.

Pilgrim) We have collectively read about noetic prayer and the nous, without really understanding it.

Hesychast) The nous is the inner man, the eye of the soul. It is our image of God, our rational faculty. It is the "boss" who rules over our person, and it is situated within our physical heart....

Pilgrim) Forgive me. You just said that the nous must descend to chest level. But how can it descend to our chest if it is already there?

Hesychast) I was about to explain that the conceptual images and thoughts which rise to the head, as Jesus our Lord disclosed to us, are also called "nous". There is also another definition of nous, that of the subtlest attention which pours out of the nous at the heart as we awaken. Therefore, the inner man or eye of the soul - the essence of the nous - is found at the heart, and the thoughts and attention are the energy coming out of there.

Pilgrim) Hmm, so the nous is really in the heart. This is our mind which begets all of our thoughts.

Hesychast) Yes, and its energy rises up to the head. We try to have it go back down to its source by way of our attention. The attention is THAT nous which returns to the heart

100

whence it came, so that the imagination will disperse, and the thoughts disappear.

Pilgrim) Is this what we read in the books about the "return of the nous to the heart?"

Hesychast) What it means is the "return of the *attention* to the heart". You see? Let us say there is a power plant in town which produces electricity. This energy comes to your home, you flip a switch, and there you have it: your computer works. If this energy was to return to the power source, your computer shuts off.

Pilgrim) So this is the descent of the mind... as we have read in St. Theophan the Recluse?

Hesychast) Most definitely. Now, this attention which must descend and adhere somewhere at the place where the physical heart is located, or somewhere close by, can also be characterized as the consciousness, awareness, or focus.

Pilgrim) Please once again?

Hesychast) OK. The nous/essence at the heart is attentive, conscious, aware and focused - it knows everything. Because part of its substance pours out throughout the body and gathers information.

Pilgrim) Where do the senses come into play in this scenario?

Hesychast) Good question. According to the neptic Saints, the energy pours out from the heart through the senses. This spirit is found all over the flesh and it gathers information, as I have mentioned, which the senses transport back to the nous at the heart. The inner man or "boss" - the nous - is at the control center, the headquarters, and from there come all the directions, questions, answers, and decisions which follow by way of thoughts and feelings.

Pilgrim) Can you explain the analogy of the power plant once again?

Hesychast) The energy coming out of our power plant at the heart is the nous/attention needed to work our brains. When we take this attention away from the head, the imaginative faculty at our head shuts off and the devil is unable to assault us with this and that thought. We simply cannot follow what he is saying or doing because our focus is concentrated elsewhere.

Pilgrim) How clever. Can I ask you father, can we still think when our nous is at the heart?

Hesychast) Of course. Haven't you heard of people coming out of a coma and they remember everything that happened when they were in that state? A man still thinks without the rubbish trying to distract him from talking to his Maker because the fantasy malfunctions.

Pilgrim) I just remembered what you said earlier about the mind leaving the externals.

Hesychast) Sure. The mind/nous is brought within and is able to connect with God, Who, by the way, resides in the heart of an orthodox person since baptism. And this way it unites. It is a beautiful thing. Then a composite thought stained by passion becomes simple and God-loving.

Pilgrim) Does the nous have to unite?

Hesychast) It is the only way to bring undistractedness. And when the focus remains intact for long periods of time the mind takes a breather from the accursed provocation and is cleansed, little by little.

Pilgrim) Is fantasy the only way by which evil thoughts manifest?

Hesychast) My elder used to tell us that no sin occurs in deed if an evil thought does not precede it by means of the imagination. To attain purity in the full sense of the word the nous must be freed from evil thoughts, from which evil and

102

passionate feelings originate. These passionate feelings cause the body to be sensually excited.

Pilgrim) And then the heart gets polluted, and it easily becomes a captive to passions and lusts?

Hesychast) Exactly. So again, in order to keep our thoughts simple and to prevent the muddiness of bad thoughts along with the stench, rising to our head, we take the nous down to the heart, we focus there, pray there, and the prayer, from being cerebral, it becomes heartfelt. That is, we start to pray with some emotion which is a necessary ingredient to pure prayer.

Pilgrim) You have mentioned a technique to go by. Can you tell us about it?

Hesychast) There are several techniques, actually, and methods which a monk uses to help him concentrate when praying with the Prayer of Jesus. But you know, God gives prayer. Without God we can do nothing.

Pilgrim) What must one do? What are some steps, before acquiring the prayer of the heart?

Hesychast) Honor the parents, confession, chastity of thought, meek behavior, partaking of Holy Communion after a proper evaluation, living simply. Then we mention "nous", to know what this is, so that we will not go astray thinking that this prayer is some strange exercise...

Pilgrim) Please go on.

Hesychast) Some people have this distorted idea of noetic prayer: about a very mysterious and complex, a way out-of-the-ordinary experience.

Pilgrim) The books and our teachers today have us believe this.

Hesychast) It seems so at first. That is why in the beginning of this journey to find the prayer of the Holy Fathers we start by reading The Way of the Pilgrim and have the Jesus Prayer repeated orally and, do you know? By saying the Holy Name of Jesus the mind is enlightened, it becomes light and agile in defending against indecent imagery.

Pilgrim) This is definitely true.

Hesychast) Well now, the breath follows the airway passage into the lung area where the heart rests. As we breathe in, we join the prayer to the air inhaled and we bring it along with our nous/focus/attention into our chest. Where the breath stops, this is where our heart is. We breathe in "Lord Jesus Christ," and breathe out "have mercy on me," after we have concentrated our attention-focus at the spot where the breath stops, by our lungs.

Pilgrim) This breathing method is widely known but its significance escapes our understanding.

Hesychast) The breath as the air goes in and out of the chest is mechanical, done always, on its own. When one joins the Jesus Prayer to it, the prayer then becomes automatic. This is a beautiful thing. And if the nous adheres to the heart, God takes over this whole function.

Pilgrim) I am trying this, but I cannot find the heart by feeling as I would my hand for instance.

Hesychast) Let us now breathe into our lung area and stop there. Okay? Now as we hold the breath, we say the prayer several times. Then we exhale. Good. Do this again: breathe in, hold the breath, say the prayer. After doing this a few times the nous, which has penetrated in there, will start to feel the greater area of the heart.

Pilgrim) What advantages does this prayer provide to those who practice it?

Hesychast) Beside undistractedness, I would say: clarity of thinking, right behavior, zeal of faith, a clean heart, and joy.

104

These are some of the advantages of praying in one's heart. Wisdom is another plus because God is in the heart, so a man becomes wise to things concerning Him.

Pilgrim) I am personally thinking back to what you said about the nous. I thought this was the intellect.

Hesychast) Let me see. In some books the nous is defined as intellect, but then the concept of the descent of the nous to the heart just remains incomprehensible. The translators are probably trying to figure out the purpose of this prayer, from an intellectual perspective. The simplicity of it is mind-boggling to many others also.

Pilgrim) I am being tripped up by this notion of the nous being in our thoughts and considerations.

Hesychast) This is because of the popular belief that we think with our brains. Do not forget that intellectual upbringings are only a product of the mind, not the mind itself. When we shut off our thinking process, the intellect vanishes as if it had never existed. The nous is the mind, which thinks and figures things out, and this nous is in the heart.

Pilgrim) I think you are right. Rational productions themselves have no ground to stand.

Hesychast) Yes. All these and the thoughts exist temporarily even though they carry demonic energy that does harm. The nous has substance and is connected to the senses so attention can be realized. The return of this nous / attention is attained by sensation. Also, since we think with our hearts to begin with, why then do we need the intellect in our head to return to the heart?

Pilgrim) Why is the essence of the nous sometimes called "the heart?"

Hesychast) To differentiate it from the energy of the nous which is in the head. When man is asleep, the spirit of the nous is solely in his heart. Then, when he awakens a chunk of it instantly fills his head. This is nous, too, and of the same substance as that of the nous in the heart. So, the Saints give these two a different name to distinguish one from the other.

Pilgrim) I had been confused for years with this nous idea. Why?

Hesychast) You are not Greek. In our culture when we hear "nous"" we think straight away about attention, the simple people and the educated alike. "Keep your nous on the boiling pot of water," or "put your nous to it," or "keep your nous at the mailbox." "Where is your nous?," they say. This is the same as "where is your mind?" Do you see now? What does prayer of the heart call for? "Put the attention at the heart." It is that simple.

Pilgrim) So it is all about being attentive and focused on our physical heart. Is that all?

Hesychast) Yes, unlike the intellect, the nous/attention, or focus, or awareness uses the senses to move about going from one limb to the other, from the stomach to the knee, to the arm. It has something to hold on to. When going to sleep, it goes back to the heart to rest.

Pilgrim) I have a silly question: when the nous goes back to the heart, are we going to sleep?

Hesychast) It is reasonable to ask such a question. We do not concentrate all of our nous at the heart but only 50% initially. Our consciousness at the head does not shut off. On the contrary, we are more alert than ever. The imagination shuts off, not the brain. So, we are not going back to sleep. Some of our attention is below the neck, enough that the imaginative faculty cannot so readily produce images.

Pilgrim) That makes sense, can we drink some coffee to be more alert?

Hesychast) Coffee is recommended. Alertness must be 100% for the prayer to work. What we are trying to accomplish here is to be undistracted, not to go on a hayride. A state of being half-asleep promotes demonic activity because the guard is down.

Pilgrim) What about deception. Is that a factor at all?

Hesychast) In a human being, matter and spirit coexist. So, this sort of thing is all around us: we live in it. Who can claim today that he is "all there?" We are ill and subject to falling into a madness at any moment. A man who cannot come to terms with this truth already lives in a delusional state. We continually slip in and out of the Spirit world, we are angels at one point and then quickly we turn into demons.

Pilgrim) How true that is; our mind changes and becomes like one or the other.

Hesychast) You know, those little devils come close, and we cannot see them. But just because we could succumb to a temptation at any moment, and so quickly, we cannot stop praying within our heart. Billions have prayed this way, mystically One-on-one with the Lord. A man can go insane without cause today, but not by saying the Jesus Prayer inside himself.

Pilgrim) To pray with the heart is to say the prayer within?

Hesychast) Of course. The inner voice says the Jesus Prayer at our command and this inner voice, by which we think and read books silently, is the voice of the heart. We give it the Lord's Name to repeat so we don't get into trouble. If the inner voice does not have something holy to say, it will blaspheme and utter all kinds of trash, and the imagination will go on the loose fighting us.

Pilgrim) But how can this happen when we love God so much and want to please Him?

Hesychast) We are going back to square one. Our nous is not in unity and is unable to control itself. Haven't you noticed? We do what we do not want to do. We say things that we do not mean. It is a mess in there. Read chapter 7 of the Epistle to the Romans: "There is another law in my members warring against the law of my mind," to quote the Apostle. If we really wanted to change, we could do it today, but...

Pilgrim) Can you tell us more about this voice of the heart and how it works?

Hesychast) This inner voice we have is our logos. The logos expresses our heart. So, the nous in our heart has a voice, but this voice is not consistent because the nous is really fragmented and ill. The reason is the passions and the devil's malice. One moment our nous says this and then that. To become healthy, it must unite with our will so as to love God with all our mind, heart, and strength. To accomplish this unity, we give our nous Jesus' Name to recite.

Pilgrim) Is this how man comes to himself and thinks of God always?

Hesychast) You got it. This is the famous prayer of the heart: to say the Jesus Prayer within our chest, to listen intently to the holy words of the Prayer, and to do this with love. By this way, the three aspects of the soul - the nous, the logos, and the spirit – unite, and man thus unites with God as St. Gregory Palamas has stated.

Pilgrim) But we cannot have distractions fighting us when we are trying to pray.

Hesychast) That is right. In time, as we progress saying the Prayer always, sometimes vocally and other times inwardly, the heart will begin to repeat the Jesus Prayer of its own accord. But as you said, we cannot have distractions fighting

108

us, so, during our personal prayer time, we drop our nous (our attention, that is) to heart level and pray there.

Pilgrim) Please elucidate this matter once more. We do this to unite our soul, you said?

Hesychast) When the attention is below the neck, the various evil thoughts springing out of the heart, turn from composite - I mean fueled by the passions and fantasy - to simple and innocent. We are then able to give all of ourselves to God.

Pilgrim) You said: nous, logos and spirit. What is this spirit you are referring to?

Hesychast) These three powers of the soul are the image of God in humans. The nous, as I have already told you, is the eye of the soul, its purest part. It is contained in the heart. This nous begets our thoughts which the logos expresses in words and conceptual images, and the spirit of the soul gives life to the body.

Pilgrim) So the nous is in the heart and it thinks, figures out, and decides what to do?

Hesychast) The nous itself has three aspects: Desire, Volition, and Intelligence. It desires mainly to be united with God but as a person grows, it picks up other desires and passions of the flesh and is not able or willing to be united with the One who created it. There is a civil war within the soul. On the one hand the desire to be with God, and on the other hand all the vices - as desires - which are instigated by the evil one to stop the nous in its ascent toward God.

Pilgrim) Is this the other law in our members which St. Paul wrote about in Romans chapter 7?

Hesychast) I think this is the law of the flesh. We come into bad habits, and they become passions which fight within our nous. Our Intelligence, or Cognition, wants to go to church but our Volition or Willpower is not strong enough to get our Desire

109

out of bed. Or a man desires to quit smoking, but the Intelligence does not, so our Willpower does not act. Or the Cognition / Intelligence knows that what the Desire wants is sinful, but it takes time for it to persuade the Volition / Incensive aspect that it should hate this desire. Or the Incensive aspect gets upset and starts condemning someone, the Cognition reacts because it reasons that this goes against God's law, but the Desire does not care.

Pilgrim) There is a conflict in all of us, I agree. You are right father. Please continue.

Hesychast) Since our nous, because of this conflict, cannot agree with itself, the logos, or inner voice, sometimes says this and sometimes says that. We change every minute according to different appetites, thoughts and feelings. And we also have the tempter...

Pilgrim) I understand. This is a very difficult situation.

Hesychast) Surely. It is like having three people living in this house - the nous - and when dinnertime comes, they go their own way. One of them takes the food to his room, the other goes to watch the ball game, and the third stays in the kitchen all alone. Ignoble activities of the fantasy do not help in this.

Pilgrim) What is the connection between this misbehavior and the faculty of the imagination?

Hesychast) This faculty is the troublemaker who calls and texts and tries to keep the powers of the nous separated so there is dissension at home. It sends provocative images to the appetitive/desiring aspect to stir things up and then it's like cats and dogs in there with an angered Volition throwing a fit, and the Cognition trying to make sense of this.

Pilgrim) You said that all this strife and anguish is expressed through the logos?

Hesychast) Yes. You notice how confused you are at times and all of a sudden you start yelling for no reason? Your inner voice has gone berserk, simply because your nous is a broken home, with no peace, no agreement and no stability. The thoughts which spring out of the inner voice come out of an ailing heart and they make no sense at all.

Pilgrim) I'm at a loss. Tell us then, one more time, how to bring agreement and stability back home.

Hesychast) To bring back the love into the "home" of the nous, we must eliminate the fantasy which brings up all the trash of the memory and presents it to our mind. The devil's main weapons are the pictures which disturb the soul and confuse it. When we close the devil's outreach program - we do this with noetic prayer - our powers start to find peace and they start getting along.

Pilgrim) So again, the return of the nous to the heart plays the key role in this?

Hesychast) The movement of the nous toward the physical heart destroys the fantasy. We are diverting a good portion of our attention from its natural course of heart-to-head, and by feeling our heart we bring this attention, or focus, you could say, back to the heart where it sprang out of. Fantasy then disperses into thin air along with all the evil thoughts and distractions.

Pilgrim) This, I feel, is too easy to be true. I thought of this prayer as something mystical.

Hesychast) You and thousands of other people who are caught up with secret esoteric systems, unattainable experiences, lights, and strange phenomena. These are not prayer of the heart. All we are trying to do is to be attentive to the words of our prayers because this burns our common enemy. We are trying to gather ourselves to pray with feeling and love toward our Lord and Savior.

Pilgrim) And I, too, thought that with this return we bring back the reason of the nous within us, or some other incredible thing.

Hesychast) As far as reason goes, the heart does not need the brain to reason. The intellect in our head reasons but it is swayed at the same time by passions, so our logical opinions, ideas and things are tainted by demonic energy. But when we reason in our heart the thoughts stay simple without the hue of the passions.

Pilgrim) I see. So, we can logically think with the nous in the heart. Is that right?

Hesychast) Correct. Again, there is nothing to bring back to our heart but our nous/attention. The powers of our soul and all the rational and physical aspects are in our heart already, they are not going anywhere. What we have to do is to be attentive and aware of what we are saying when we pray, because this is the problem. When we finally find stillness of thought, God's grace enlightens us, and we feel good, holy and our conscience approves.

Pilgrim) Can you tell us something about the conscience and how it works? We don't hear so much about it.

Hesychast) As far as I know, our being includes a body, a soul and what the Fathers call a "spirit" - which is our conscience - that God gave us to know that He exists and as a compass to find our way to His Kingdom. This conscience is the voice of God to know Him, to love Him, to connect with Him, the One Who Is. In chapter 2 of the Gospel of St. John it says that the Word enlightens every man that comes into the world. I would think the Word does so by the conscience which is His law and the knowledge that He exists. St. Diadochos of Photiki says that God dwells in our conscience.

Pilgrim) I would like to ask something: did you say, Father, that the nous in the heart and the nous in the head are of one essence?

Hesychast) You know it. Like the heat in the fireplace and the heat up at the chimney. We think in our heart, and we think in our head the same thoughts. Except that when the thoughts reach the head, they become complex, as I said, because of the fantasy. The organ of imagination, St. John Damascene wrote, is the anterior ventricle of the brain. Because of our memory and the hatred of the demons, the imagination takes us down.

Pilgrim) What other methods can we use to stop fantasy?

Hesychast) When we pull a prayer rope with our fingers as we repeat the Jesus Prayer, that helps. When we listen intently upon holy words of the Prayer this is also huge, and gratitude to our Benefactor who gives us so much each day. To thank the Lord for all things, we forget this. Cry out the prayer, my boys, there is no other Name in heaven, and hell, and on earth.

Pilgrim) Thank you so much. Please bless us now so we can return safely to our homes.

Hesychast) May the Lord bless you abundantly through the prayers of my elder. Amen. Have a safe trip and remember my lowliness in your prayers. Try to pray noetically and then do come back someday, by the will of God.

Student) Good evening. Welcome to our program, your Reverence. Tonight, we would like for you to expand our horizons in regard to the topic of prayer and the effect it has on the soul.

Deacon) Thank you for the opportunity. Today, man's soul is ailing and in need of a strong prayer and reflection upon the things concerning God. I see that we have the time and because we address a wider audience, we may go more in depth... well, the subject in question intensifies our longing to know God better since we are His image. Therefore, when we come to know ourselves, this reflects into our understanding a more complete view of the Prototype - Jesus - by whom we have attained our formation.

Student) You always introduce your students to the dual make up of body and soul. You seem to begin there. Tell us about it.

Deacon) Sure. Some of the human body's functions and powers resemble those of other mammals along with the bestial instincts of nourishment, reproduction, and self-preservation. But man's body commands or obeys the soul and because of their union there is either dissension or agreement between them. This occurrence does not take place in the animal kingdom because the souls of animals are unlike those of humans. I commence all my classes by bringing up this distinction. We differ considerably from other creatures who act according to natural laws pertaining to each kind. For mankind the leash is long, to put it mildly, and we get in trouble doing unnatural things where either our body or soul disapproves.

Student) And why does this happen?

Deacon) Man is free and rational and does whatever he wants. Because of the devil's influence he is swayed like a pendulum in regard to decision-making. Half of the time he doesn't know what he is doing. The other half he's asleep. I say that no one should despair over this condition. But to have an idea of who we are, this is a good thing. The ancients used to say, "know thyself."

Student) The fact is hard to swallow, yet how true your words are. We are ill and in need of healing; we should know this.

Deacon) The knowledge that we succumb to temptation and fall every day, will bring us to confession and break the bonds of sin, in time. Let us then go a little deeper to see ourselves better. Afterward by way of self-reproach we will start being aware that the fault lies within, not in other people. As it happens often, this shall draw the grace of God, and one may enter spheres of yet much higher knowledge. Now, the human soul is endowed with grace since its conception. This is the breath of God given to us as the divine image which includes a conscience and a rational faculty and with these we are enlightened as to how we should live and think.

Student) Tell us about the conscience. What is it?

Deacon) The conscience is God's voice. It serves as a compass to help us find His Kingdom by being good and virtuous people. It insists on it and it's quick to reprove and censure unless our thoughts and deeds are aligned with its propensity. It is also said that the conscience is God's Law, or that the Law of God was given to a man's conscience, and that the conscience is a man's natural or innate Holy Scripture; it is his "Bible" or as others say: "The tablets of the Law."

Student) What about the rational faculty that you spoke of? And how does it function?

Deacon) This is our mind or what the Greek fathers call the "nous." The mind is spirit and thus it has spiritual vision. When it listens and obeys the conscience it is able to apprehend and quickly comes to an understanding of higher things and is discerning of the divine, earthly or demonic. But when this mind does not pay heed to God's messages, it is darkened, and ignorance obscures its apprehension and understanding. Besides this, it loses its acuteness and quick-wittedness. So now, as we draw closer to the topic of prayer we'll see that prayer is very important. Prayer is the mind's bread and butter, the nourishment it needs to survive. Yet, to be fully realized the soul's "peptic" system must be healthy and strong.

Student) What do you mean?

Deacon) Prayer is communication between the creature, little man, and Infinite God. And it feeds him like a mother does her baby who cannot do without her. But speaking for each of us as a prodigal son, and having become used to feeding on things of the world – the food for swine – when we repent and we come back to the Father, it happens that sometimes we need time to adjust, for our system to make the transition, from the pods we were used to, to the fresh and wholesome spiritual food…

Student) I understand now. Forgive me for the interruption. You are saying that a beginner must take baby steps, if I am correct.

Deacon) Exactly. First comes the "milk" of repentance, that is, heartfelt prayer which gives birth to remorse for sin. And so, the fear of God is begotten. The fear of God then begets temperance, temperance begets patience, and patience begets hope. Meanwhile the prayer becomes strong and, by the hope as its ally, dispassion is attained. So, there are stages one must go through to arrive at this point, and it could take many years, if at all. Strangely enough, a take-it-slow approach to

116

this endeavor of a spiritual variety produces much quicker and better results.

Student) So we must not hurry at this juncture. This is good and necessary, to go slow at first. But why? Please elaborate.

Deacon) This is the way one must travel in order to acquire knowledge and skill. If this is the case in the secular world, so much more it is appropriate to follow a spiritual course painstakingly for it is a minefield out there; we cannot see the little devils and what they are up to. The best way to do it is to take it a step at a time - all of us - and see where this way will lead, by God's grace. If we are serious about our faith, we should also come to feel the need to receive counsel from others who have more experience and have gone through this field successfully.

Student) And this is what we are doing now, Professor. We are here to learn.

Deacon) Yes. Since man has freedom to choose and do whatever but inclines oftentimes toward doing unnatural things where afterwards his body or soul disapproves, as mentioned, we start there. Our heart, which is the primary spiritual organ, sometimes leans on doing good and natural things, but at times it gets entangled in craving sins and then it aches as our stomach would ache if it was obliged to digest wood shavings. Why then does our heart ache after committing a sin? Because our conscience is stirred up and starts nagging. You see? So go ahead and try to pray afterward, if you can...

Student) Please continue. This is very interesting.

Deacon) What I am saying is that we have reins to control our behavior. Our mind cannot just do whatever it wishes. I have pointed this out several times so far in our discussion and I aim to continue shedding light upon the fact that there must be agreement on a deeper level so that prayer is fully realized.

We should consume good things; fresh wholesome "food" so that we can acquire a taste for virtue. Everything will be ok after we do this.

Student) What if we make a mistake and fall into a sin? What then?

Deacon) We run to confession. It is very simple. The mystery of repentance mends our relationship with our Maker who easily forgets our transgressions, looks the other way, and patiently waits so that we get back on track. Then, as we are praying we feel His loving presence permeates our entire being. But... after a while we unfortunately forget God's love and we are thus liable to commit the same sin. Again, we go to confession, we are forgiven and then we fall. After this, back to confession, and so on. It's a cycle.

Student) What role does the devil play in all this?

Deacon) He doesn't leave a man at peace. He wants to see squabbles, dissension, disagreement and tension between the conscience and the mind of the poor fellow. It's funny that at the seminary we are required to teach subjects such as orthodox theology, the sacred dogmas and the canons, sacramental theology, distinctions between the created and uncreated, ecclesiastical calendars and new year's, ecumenical councils, deification of man, personal transformation and renewal, etc., but not much, if anything, on the soul and one's mind. And who needs a conscience? We leave it for after we die, unfortunately.

Student) Tell us, how does the devil fight us? And what are his main weapons?

Deacon) The evil one is not absolute spirit like God but has an immaterial body that is akin to the Soul. He approaches a person silently and imparts to him what he has: darkness, fears, anxiety, depression - a demon is all this. Now, a man who sets straight his conscience with regular confession is enlightened and feels the danger. He knows what this dark spirit is "selling" and chases him away with rebuttal and the Jesus Prayer. By the way, this awesome prayer, "Lord Jesus Christ have mercy on me," is the most effective weapon that a man uses against the devil. And the devil's weapons are the evil thoughts which go up in smoke when pitted against the Divine Name.

Student) Alright. We need a clear conscience. And then the Jesus Prayer to take care of the thoughts. Let me ask, your Reverence, how do we protect ourselves, so the dark one does not approach us at all?

Deacon) Good question. This, my good friend, is the ideal. For this we need watchfulness which is the guarding of the mind or nous. So, yes, a clear conscience is the key and the mind then enters another sphere of insight. It starts seeing things that had escaped its understanding previously. Now it sees clearly and discerns inner movements independently of its passions, and without much effort, it puts them in their place, whether in storage for later use, or casts them into the abyss of oblivion.

Student) Hmm, how important is watchfulness. I am starting to realize this now.

Deacon) Watchfulness, or vigilance, or guarding of the nous surpasses many virtues. By Christ's power the guarding of this faculty can change men from being indecent, profane, ignorant, unjust, to being pure, holy, wise and just. Beyond these things, by the guarding of one's mind, a Christian becomes capable of theologizing. Also, by the guarding of his mind, a holy hesychast sees the mysteries of God that other mortals are unable to see.

Student) I like the concept of watchfulness. But I'm not a monk. How does a sinner like me make a start?

Deacon) Well... clean up your act. Sometimes I come across folks who love to pray. Yet, they cannot change their ways, nor do they want to. A man who strives to get on higher level but does not take care to limit the intake of inappropriate data, is like a man who is trying to make a hole in the water. Of course you have to forgive me; I did not mean to offend. Now listen to this: the mind is a spirit – in patristics, as I have mentioned, it is called "nous" – and this spirit cannot in any way be identified as the brain. The brain is flesh, the mind is spirit. Remember that.

Student) Excuse me deacon. Please do explain this spirit idea for our listeners?

Deacon) The mind/nous cannot be seen by the naked eye. It is not like anything tangible. The elements of which it is formed are unknown to science. Its essence is something unique and ethereal and since antiquity it has been sheltered by a veil of mystery. This spirit along with the conscience is the grace poured upon the soul by the breath of God to make it a "living soul." We talked about this earlier...

Student) Please continue.

Deacon) The great neptics call the nous, to use this term, the "eye of the soul." These are the Saints who wrote about watchfulness. They refer to two major components of this work which interplay and complement each other once a virtuous lifestyle is incorporated into a man's daily routine. The first component is a razor-sharp attention, and the second the prayer to Jesus. We talked only briefly of the Jesus Prayer, the value of which is priceless because of Christ's Holy Name. So, the attention guards the eye of the soul zealously and with the use of the Jesus prayer it sends evil thoughts to ruin.

Student) Well, we thank you, teach', we conclude from your discourse this evening that prayer is greatly influenced by one's disposition and character. Is this not the case?

Deacon) It is definitely. The topic of prayer, though it be inexhaustible in nature, can be condensed to fit a wallet. And like a credit card pulled out of there, it is backed by a mountain of gold, that being the love for God and neighbor. Without this currency all works are for the garbage disposal.

Student) What of the effect prayer might have on one's soul? This is that other part belonging to the subject of our discussion, I think that now is a good time for you to comment.

Deacon) Yes.... It is natural for all peoples in all cultures and traditions to seek and to find the lost Paradise. So, what is the effect that all of us are looking for when we pray? That perfect state of being in the Garden of Eden. Let us not lie to ourselves and talk about coping with ascesis, adversity and pains as the end of our struggle in Christ. These are only means. The end is that peace and feeling of joy that goes through us when we taste His love and we exclaim: "Thank you Lord, for you are benevolent and kind. Thank you! Thank you!"

Student) Please share with us a final thought.

Deacon) Remember, son: even though it seems that God allows us to pick and choose and do whatever we want, still, He is in control; He is the admiral on our "ship." Under Him is the captain, our conscience, who is at the helm and cannot let this vessel veer off course. Our mind - the sailor boy - is under obedience; he has someone to answer to. Let us not think for a minute that our mind is independent and able to set out and sail the seven seas. It must obey, you got it? You don't want to have your conscience get all riled up is what I'm saying. This is a big mistake. And that goes for all of us. There is a big price to pay for mutiny - who wants to walk the plank? I don't want my mind to end up with the sharks - those ugly demons - who rip and devour their prey. So, you know what? Let me be good and holy, and obedient, climbing the mast to set the sails, mopping floors, and making grub. The helmsman will then be happy and so will our master, and prayer will come to soothe the soul like a gentle breeze as we arrive safely into harbor. This is how one gets prayer. By being obedient and loyal. Then joy and contentment follow. You know, cause and effect.

Student) We thank you so much. Have a good night.

Spiritual Tips

- *Call on the Theotokos in times of need: Panagia, save me!*
- *The person determined to lead a spiritual life must understand that he is ailing. "Know thyself," said the ancients.*
- *If, by chance, you give assent to evil thoughts, know that the tempter is around. Repent quickly to ward him off.*
- *Do not be obsessed with how you feel. Think of those who are naked, hungry, in jail, in hospitals, nursing homes, etc.*
- *Adversity promotes mental and physical health.*

Pilgrim) Your blessing Father-Abbot, we have come from Canada on a trip and looked up your monastery. Do you have some time?

Abbot) Of course, my children. We receive all and we find time to spend if they like to talk about something of a spiritual nature. But first, let us go to church to venerate the saints and pray.

Pilgrim) Father, we are Serbian Orthodox living in the diaspora for some decades now. If you please, give us a word of wisdom. Tell us how we can improve our position before God.

Abbot) (smiles) You already have. Do you see? As soon as you came through our gates. I see that you fear God - oh, Michael... welcome. Come into the refectory, sit with the others, here by me. In this changing world, my dear ones, you must find time and search to find yourselves. We all have only one soul and one life to live on earth to prepare for eternity.

Pilgrim) And how do we go about doing that?

Abbot) You prepare by prayer, fasting, confession to a priest, almsgiving, things like that. Your heart knows what to do. We all have a conscience - the voice of God - there is no escaping Him. Divine counsels are man's bread and butter. In the gospel of St. John, in the first chapter I think it says that the Word enlightens every man that comes into the world. And I think by the conscience does God enlighten his rational creatures. And He censures them when he has to.

Pilgrim) Don't we all know that! But why do we still always fall? I mean, every day.

Abbot) Take a moment and picture yourself driving down the highway as a police vehicle is following you. And it continues to follow after half a kilometer or so as you now make sure that your seatbelt is on, the speed is right, your hands on the wheel. So why do you forget, all of you, that God is watching. Do you even care?

Pilgrim) Shame on us. We so easily forget.

Abbot) Shame? Obviously this is not an issue. If you were on the street in the heart of Sydney committing a crime I can see that, but here we are talking about no mere passerby but the Law-Maker Himself who can throw you in jail, literally. To be ashamed before people is something, but to have the Almighty present as sin is being committed in thought, word or deed this is something else. Men blatantly curse, kill, lie, fornicate, without any scruples. What do you mean by shame? If you had any shame... well, I for one, we are all in the same pot - the world would be a better place...

Pilgrim) I guess you put us in our place, Father. But please do tell us how we can improve to make Him more real in our lives, and so to be more readily ashamed.

Abbot) The feeling of God's presence must be at the top of the heap among virtues an Orthodox Christian strives to attain. You said it: "to make Him more real." Therefore, the topic of reality is of paramount importance - it is the premium fuel to use for your spiritual engine. And if you want a long-lasting output, mix in the additive of patience to this reality: that God is watching you. what did the prophet said in his Psalm: "I have You always before me so I will not sway." All the Saints did this: they struggled against evil, with faith and patience.

Pilgrim) So this is the faith of the Saints and the Holy Fathers?

Abbot) Yes, this faith begets the idea that we are NEVER alone; this is the truth of it all. This is the cornerstone, if you will. And the patience is the mortar needed to bind it all together so our building will not collapse. Jesus is the cornerstone that the pharisees disregarded. He said: "By your patience possess your souls." You see? Have your eyes on the Lord and have patience. Well, it is easier said than done, that's a fact.

Pilgrim) Is this how the monks in your monastery do battle against themselves and against our common enemy?

Abbot) The faith that God and His sweet Mother are around here in our place of repentance watching our every move, keeps us in check, always on the lookout for trouble, mostly. If a bad thought enters the scope of our spiritual expanse, we must quickly apprehend it lest we offend God and lose His favor. There is a price to pay, my friends, for giving asylum to demonic thoughts and their associates, such as the schemes and behind-the-scenes intrigue connected with this type of rubbish. When we neglect to come to a complete halt at a stop sign - watch out! Or if we speed recklessly. Then the lights will be on our back, and the sirens, and of course the ticket in the hand.

Pilgrim) What sort of penalty do we expect to receive for our various cases of misconduct?

Abbot) It is different for each one. Don't forget: God is love but also justice. He has set up laws and by-laws, courts of appeal, and tribunals, of a spiritual kind. And the punishment or fine imposed must be carried out and it is carried out - there is not much you can do except pray and of course repent. If by repenting before a worldly magistrate to be freed of liability does the job, then there is hope that repenting before an Orthodox priest will work - partially - until the debt is paid off. There must be a punishment, the spiritual mirror the earthly. God, therefore, penalizes each offender but He does this with discretion. He wants the penitent to come to himself by using his or her conscience, putting it to work and by being attentive, through the rear-view mirror, of the squad car

125

following him. This is what the holy men and hermits do always. They watch out.

Pilgrim) When the conscience is stirred up, this means trouble. I am saying this because I feel it sometimes. We have to be "all eyes."

Abbot) The conscience is what our Lord refers to when He tells us to make peace with our adversary on the way to judgement. This is going to be our worst enemy, it is the unsleeping worm crawling inside an unrepentant man after death. Now in this life, a fellow can take sleeping pills, fly to Hawaii to escape, drink or do drugs to forget his sins, or just plain don't listen to his conscience until it stops reproving him. But after death there is no repentance, no place to escape. It will be dreadful.

Pilgrim) Did the fathers really put as much effort as we all do today to curb their lusts and passions?

Abbot) I will tell you: books, many of which are misleading, present Saints who did not fight with their passions, like they dropped out of the sky. As if they were born a saint. This is a problem. Regular people cannot identify with this. We are all humans. There is the example of Cain who had not learned to hurt others by any example beforehand. Yet he killed his brother. So, this explains to us and as it is written: that we all incline toward evil since our youth. We are not primordial man before the fall. The sin is innate in us, we are ill, and unlike our first parents, we do not see the snakes of evil desires, propensities, notions and lusts but we have their roots in our hearts and the evil one fights us now from the inside, with imaginings pertaining to these thoughts...

Pilgrim) Forgive me. We have read of desert dwellers - the neptics - who are fighting back. They watch out, as you have mentioned. It's funny, we were talking about this in the van on the way here. Could you explain?

126

Abbot) The term nepsis means watchfulness or vigilance - to put the attention at the place where the thoughts first appear, basically. But I must stress again: the fear which is so important to have. And not just fear that we'll offend Jesus, but to be initially afraid that we could be punished and put to the shackles in prison for all eternity. So, the holy ones, my children, are aware that they have been followed all along by God, for He is actively pursuing them. He lays down the law. So, they go through a great deal of trouble to keep Him happy...

Pilgrim) Please do continue.

Abbot) God loves us so much. It is written somewhere in the Good Book that a father disciplines those he loves, and so it makes sense that our Father in heaven will get His way, or else! What parent will not take precautions so that their child does not "take the wrong road?" Our dear Lord went on the cross for us, He cares. And He gave us Scripture and the prophets, the Apostles and Saints, and now in the later years He gave us monks who were able to decipher - by their way of life - the written works of such luminaries as Sts. Maximos the Confessor and Gregory Palamas, the dean of the great Hesychasts. So here it is: Watchfulness - to be attentive of one's heart from where evil emerges, so that with God's help, you, or everyone interested, may shuffle away quickly thoughts which annoy and disturb the soul.

Pilgrim) And you said to start from the fear of God's presence. And then to be aware of thoughts.

Abbot) Exactly. First things first. Keep your eyes on the road and you will avoid all trouble in time. If a man wants to get somewhere - in any endeavor - he must get there in one piece. So let us abide as if our Savior's gaze is upon us at all times, to feel safe; have His memory in mind, to stay within the lines. Then let us not imagine things because fantasy is the bridge of the demons. In order to sin, the mind is assaulted by a conceptual image which stirs the passions within. The image itself carries an idea by which a correlating thought is produced to entice the senses.

Pilgrim) But how do we stop fantasy since it is - as many believe - such an integral part of our composition?

Abbot) You are so right. We need the faculty of imagination to aspire, hope, create. It is essentially a must-have to be able to function in this world. But as we all know, the intrusive thoughts that are dressed inappropriately must be shown the door as soon as they are detected. This is what I meant when I said, "let's not imagine". Our thinking mechanism is not at fault but our passion which wants something bad to look at - yes, don't let this surprise you. We like it! The nous of man has the power to put a *logismos*, a passionate thought that is, away before it materializes into something obscene. But it just stands there as an accomplice. After this, the wheels are coming off, you know what I mean? The ambulance arrives, and the paramedics with the excuses to bandage you up... The next day you wake up with a 'hangover'. Oh, now I have to go to confession.

Pilgrim) It's déjà vu. You are talking about me, Father... But now, if you can, decode your words for us. I feel that there is more to this. So please go on, give us the scoop.

Abbot) I will. Of course, I am not referring to alcohol - you are not drinkers. I have been using the analogy of the memory of our Lord as the patrolman following closely behind. That should help anyone to "steer" away from trouble. But since it is hard to do this always, you need a friend for support, a co-driver so to speak. You need the Noetic Prayer "Lord Jesus Christ have mercy on me." So, your mind, or what the Greeks

128

call nous, is at the helm and the nous driving your vehicle down life's boulevard is affected by some inner and outer components...

Pilgrim) I am beginning to understand. But please keep going, we appreciate your input.

Abbot) Outside influences that can affect a soul in a negative way are: wrong friends or coworkers, vulgar expressions and imagery, indecent cinema, and bad weather, to mention a few. But we will not linger here. If we had to examine only these influences, we could be here for hours (smiles). There is one factor though, which plays a leading role in all this, and that is the appetitive aspect of the nous, also called Desire. The nous/mind desires and, more often than not, it begets thoughts according to its tastes and whims, or rather the passing fancies instigated by the demons that appear from without to capture one's attention.

Pilgrim) Most of us are familiar with this aspect as well as the other two: the Cognitive or Intelligent, and the Incensive or Volitional.

Abbot) Very good. You are a knowledgeable bunch... So the Desire then, when it has acquired a taste for divine things, exerts pressure on the cognitive faculty to accept concepts inspired by angels or to produce itself only holy thoughts. "I do not want to see or hear evil things," it says to its co-aspect. And, if needed, it will seek help from the Volition/Willpower to have its way. When the Desire does not budge, man is sanctified - this is how Saints are made.

Pilgrim) To only want good things. What an ideal!

Abbot) That's right, to envy a man of God and to go his way. It will get a little rough being off-road, or rather going against the traffic, and it may end up being a demolition derby - can you imagine? Most folks today are driving down Perdition

Lane so when you are headed uptown you are going to get hit, there is no avoiding it. And the little devils, they are going to be atop your car, on the hood, and hanging outside the window like monkeys as you drive through the zoo. But no worries, because you relish being with the Lord and doing His will. You know what? Now the police will be leading the way up ahead, opening up the road, and if there is some mishap where the enemy creates an incident blocking your view, well... here comes the constable on the bike.

Pilgrim) Have you seen those guys? Being so agile and quick.

Abbot) They are wiry but mean. And they know how to use that whistle; they will play you a tune. These boys are terrifying. And I will tell you because we have them here in town: their secret is that they become one with the bike (smiles). Now... to continue, I must implore you to go after good things, virtues. When you do what God wants, you come to know that God is good, wise, benevolent. And you feel good about yourself and righteous so there is nothing obstructing you from being all you can be.

Pilgrim) We do love God. Yet we have not reached the plateau of perfection. I guess this is the reason we visit monasteries. Can you help us along? How do we reach a satisfactory level?

Abbot) What did our Savior say in the gospels? To hate yourself; not to have a high opinion concerning your person. What He is really saying here is not to have excessive self-love which is the mother of all the passions. This is the ideal. But since most people cannot handle humility - you think you can huh? - then...at least start hating sin. You can do this. Again, we have the three aspects or powers of our soul: the *intelligent*, the *desiring*, and the *incensive*. So, you give your intelligent aspect the Jesus Prayer and your incensive aspect the hatred for sin. Now, the desiring aspect is stubborn and ornery. You are going to have problems at first, but this strong dislike you are displaying against vices which were once your friends and cohorts, will win in the end. Of that, you can be sure.

Pilgrim) How long will it take before we see the fruits begotten of this holy effort?

Abbot) This depends wholly on you. If you don't pay attention to the signs or cannot lay off the gas pedal, you will not go far. You are liable to end up out in the fields or in someone's front yard, at best. Keep the remembrance of the squad car following you. God loves you but not those monkeys - don't you roll the window down. The holy fathers say that if a soul wants something bad enough, it will acquire it. This is true, I have seen it myself. But I hear the bells for vespers. We will resume our talk after the evening meal.

To be continued -

Spiritual Tips

- *Two primary ways to battle egotism are through monasticism and marriage.*
- *Both monasticism and marriage are types of ascetic labor.*
- *Both battle egotism by making us responsible to others and by making us put our own needs behind the needs or wants of another (our spouse, family, Geronda, etc.).*

A FEW WORDS ON SPIRITUAL MATTERS

ON THOUGHTS

- So to be able to have fewer bad thoughts, let us give our nous (mind) a spiritual occupation, like memory of death, consciousnesses of our sinfulness, the Kingdom of God. When we are doing this, evil cannot penetrate us because we are filled with good things.
- Since thoughts are manifested by way of images which spring forth from the imaginative part of the soul, try to cleanse the fantastico (the faculty of imagination).
- To have fewer thoughts and distractions we have to simplify our lives, because the clutter of many things (material or otherwise) will clutter our mind and subsequently the cares for these things will produce stress, fear, sadness...
- With one good thought we go to heaven and with one evil thought we are in hell.

ON THE HEART

- Prayer, keeping vigil and the renunciation of worldly and unnecessary things are the means by which the heart is purified. If our heart is purified, then our thoughts will be pure also.
- But simplicity of life cannot be overlooked, being an essential part of peaceful living. If the heart desires things which are vain, vain thoughts will appear. In other words, when we live simply, we feel and we think simply.

- Whatever is in our heart appears in our head. There is a strong connection between thoughts, the heart, and vigilant attention. We need this vigilant attention to keep our heart from defilement by foul thoughts.

ON WATCHFULNESS

- The greatest temple, in which God delights to be, is that which He skillfully crafted - our entire being, our soul. But a chaste heart is needed.
- Watchfulness means close attention to thoughts, fantasies, and the movement of the senses; it is a spiritual strength that opposes evil; it is clear perception.
- To keep one's soul in a healthy condition, a watchful mind sees temptations from afar and quickly escapes the battle as it takes all safety measures.
- Nepsis (watchfulness) is when the nous (mind) oversees the heart and guards it.
- The sacrament of repentance is the most blessed of all sacraments because it provides excellent preparation for the next life.
- Shame in confession must be put aside.
- Confession abolishes death, persistent thoughts, and lessens the effect of various trials.

ON NOETIC PRAYER

- Noetic prayer is the most renowned. It consists of seven words—Lord Jesus Christ have mercy on me. This is the Jesus Prayer.

- The Holy Fathers taught us that when a soul is attacked by filthy, proud or blasphemous thoughts, it is not enough to flee the danger, but the soul must also drive away the enemy by the unceasing prayer of Jesus.
- Keep the Name of Jesus in your breath. It will teach you everything.
- The Name of Christ has restorative power within it and can return the fallen soul to a state of health and strength.
- When we "keep an eye" on our thoughts and guard the heart with watchfulness, the Jesus Prayer is guaranteed to bring results.
- Noetic prayer or prayer of the heart helps one to attain dispassion. Only this prayer is able to do this.

On Imagination

- Reverie and daydreaming are the children of an unbridled imagination.
- The *fantastico* (the faculty of imagination) is the bridge for the demons to reach over to us.
- The aim of noetic prayer is to obliterate fantasy during prayer.
- After years of struggle with sinful images and the like, when the Jesus Prayer enters the heart and Christ is enthroned within its dominion, then the prayer becomes pure, freed from all distractions.
- Distractions during prayer are evil imaginings.
- There is no sin or virtue which does not have the Imaginative faculty as its beginning and starting point.

On Love

- Do you want to see how much you love God? You will see this by how much you love your brothers. Today we are in need of love. If you catch yourself wanting to help and to pray for others, then you have love for them.
- Whoever puts himself in the place of the prisoner, the penitent, the sick, the depressed, the troubled; he offers the greatest sacrifice before God for the greatest love is to sacrifice oneself for his or her fellow man, just as our Lord did for us.
- Loving to give help and almsgiving mirror the condition of a healthy soul.
- Do not show by the countenance of your face your dislike for certain people. Struggle to love them and God will help to restore your heart in love.

On Obedience

- Obedience is memory of God and the application of His commandments.
- Obedience makes God obedient to the one who obeys.
- A loving soul is humble and obedient. The obedient are the humble.
- Obedience has the purpose of destroying the machinations of the evil one. But when we do not obey, we give room for the devil to "work".
- Our own will is the key that Christ uses to open our mind to Him. If we do not give Him the key, that is our obedience by cutting off our own will, we keep the key to ourselves and we will never succeed in anything nor will we acquire happiness.

- By feeling our physical heart, we can feel the spiritual heart contained therein, but not as in a vessel because the spirit cannot be confined or restricted.
- The spiritual heart is the nous by which men know God. The intellect in the brain, on the other hand, knows the physical world around us. These two, nous and the intellect, can proceed together.
- The movements of the spirit affect the physical heart because they are united, so when we feel the physical heart and a certain passion arouses to disturb it, without much effort we can quickly put a stop to the passion because we tangibly feel it coming by way of the sense of touch.
- The nous can feel and "touch" when it is concentrated at a certain place. Being sensitive at the physical heart, we know what is happening spiritually.
- The neptic fathers became so good at this that they knew when the passion would strike. Monks also are vigilant lest the evil one sneak in to do his damaging work unexpectedly.

136

Pilgrim) Father, you talked of the memory of God, and evil thoughts - we like them. So, is this why we fall?

Abbot) Hmm, what a pity. Yes... the devil, he knows that we make the choice; we can push him aside. That's why when we are young, he will go to a great deal of trouble to plant evil desires into our hearts. I told you earlier. When the time comes, he will strike with a thought which stirs that desire in us. Now, if this desire is a feeble habit, the willpower in us - provided that our intelligence approves - can easily subdue it and have it go back to sleep. But what if it is a strong passion that we are fond of? Now we have a problem.

Pilgrim) We see. Is this the reason we should cultivate good desires?

Abbot) Correct. We are beings of habit, and we easily like or dislike certain habits that cling to us - we let them somehow - and slowly they go into our system. In patristic literature the heart is called the "seat of desire." The heart is filled with desires. Virtues are good desires; passions are bad desires. The Church helps us to install good desires. I know I sound like a pre-school catechist, but the fact is that most people want things that are advanced without having first learned introductory things and preparatory principles. How easy it is to love God and to pray with zeal when one's heart is clean?

Pilgrim) I haven't seen the subject of watchfulness from this perspective: that if our heart were cleansed, we would not have to struggle as much.

Abbot) Surely. We talked about going uptown against the flow of traffic. It's not easy now because you are - as I see - already in your thirties, and you carry... You carry a world of ideas, inclinations, beliefs, habits which are like your back-seat driver shifting nervously, nudging your shoulder and whispering in your ear: Oh, Oh, Ohhh! Look over there! They ruffle your hair, reach forward to turn on the music - loud. And they will tell you unbelievable stories and things about goblins and fairies. Do not believe any of them. You have to know that evil thoughts are not yours. Just keep driving, say the prayer to Jesus to make them shush, and have patience.

Pilgrim) I guess we have given rights to the evil one. Is there any hope now?

Abbot) Through your mistakes there will be hope for tomorrow, for your children and your grandchildren, and for the world. Now, through hardships you will have acquired discernment, and you will protect your loved ones, so they do not go through what you went through. You will shield the children's minds from injury by giving their senses good things to desire. When they grow like this - wholesome and pure - they will be able to protect their own mind and those of their offspring, and you will receive rewards in this life and in the life to come. You can certainly clean yourself now, but it will be slower, the process that is, and cumbersome.

Pilgrim) We hear you...

Abbot) So after setting your conscience right before God with a frank confession and sincere repentance of all your transgressions, this sets the stage. And having the memory of God, and knowingly ascribing all good things to the Lord, then you take up the sword of the spirit: "Lord Jesus Christ have mercy on me." I know you do this already. But you have to say it with feeling, like you mean it. Since the devil fights you using your own desires, you are actually fighting yourself. By the Jesus Prayer, you keep down the passion, meanwhile you despise and abhor it with all your heart. In

138

other words, put it in your mind, you DO NOT want this passion. Even if you were to be led to slaughter, raise yourself once again and keep swinging. You are liable to throw a punch in there as long as you struggle, having the fear of God and dislike for the sin that mostly bothers you. Now, I know that I've been repeating myself.

Pilgrim) OK, we have to pray, and you do know that we do pray. How can we get better at prayer for a better result?

Abbot) Very good. Now we put some of the pieces together. This puzzle requires a patient effort to be filled, as I have already prescribed. Now find a place in your home to sit motionless for a quiet ten minutes. Put the Jesus Prayer on your lips and then - oh my! - you will remember about fifty things that you have to get up and do at this time: emails, lunch, the wash, groceries, to vacuum, take out the dog, get ready for work, your dentist's appointment... You have to do it now. You'll be attacked, as you probably know from your own experience. You will be attacked from all angles. So, to prevent this occurrence from taking place, prepare. How? Prepare yourself beforehand, with a sense of gratitude for all the blessings you receive daily from God. This should warm your heart.

Pilgrim) How else can we prepare?

Abbot) In the beginning there is not much you can do, except to keep saying the prayer patiently. In just a little while your head will feel like a bowl of greens with potatoes, squash, peas, something sort of a Russian salad - everything all together. You might want to walk around the room at first. Call out to Jesus with some zest and confidence that all these things ringing in your ears will dissipate. Then once the thoughts settle down, you sit...

Pilgrim) Forgive me, Father. Some of us are beyond this initial stage you are describing. Where do we go from there?

Abbot) What we are trying to accomplish by repeating the Jesus Prayer is stillness of thought, what the holy fathers call hesychia. And this first step on the ladder of prayer cannot be bypassed, nor can it ever be excluded from this venture of trying to clear the mind. Oral prayer is needed even for those who are advanced. I was told by an elder in the monastery of Philotheou on Mt Athos that, when he was younger and under obedience, it was required for the members of his brotherhood to say the prayer aloud at all times. Even for those five out of the seven brothers who went into Theoria, who experienced rapture of the nous, and saw the mysteries of God during their nightly vigil. During the day their holy elder wanted them to *say* the prayer so he could hear it.

Pilgrim) I read Patristics, but this pointer has obviously evaded my notice. Is it often the case with other minor details?

Abbot) Very much so. Modern man today wants to 'feel' the Spirit but don't talk to him about giving up the high-life and the beer. Listen my children, I have to insist that the reason the prayer said vocally does not work on the passions as well as it should is that the virtue of all virtues is not home. Again, this is purity. Make purity a value you cannot live without and watch the Jesus Prayer take over your life - boy it's sweet! You want prayer? Clean up your act. And this detail of reciting God's Name by mouth will not seem to be so minor.

Pilgrim) You seem to be hitting upon the same thing, Father. I guess it is that important.

Abbot) Forgive me. I am getting old, and it often happens that I repeat myself. But I also have to say: there is a method to my madness (smiles). And I want to help you today, I may not see you again. Since God brought you here, I had to drive this quality home. After you keep the eyes from taking into your system the filth of this world, it will be like shifting to a higher gear. Now, as you sit in your prayer corner saying the noetic Prayer of Jesus, you will try to ward off not just the bad thoughts but all your thoughts. Subsequently the mind will - in time - become accustomed to pushing away uninvited thoughts without much of an effort.

Pilgrim) We want to make the Prayer a habit.

Abbot) Exactly. The Prayer becomes something a man cannot cope without. When he stops pronouncing the Jesus Prayer he feels lost. A body is never alone when God is present. And after a bit of time the Jesus Prayer will go inside the heart to be uttered of its own accord. This is the prayer of the heart. It can happen to anyone, not just monks. When Jesus is enthroned in the heart, desire for Him consumes all the passions, and the concerns of God is all one thinks about. Everything else seems to vanish: anger, lust, envy for temporal things, greed.

Pilgrim) Could you tell us more about this phenomenon of the heart saying the prayer? It seems that you are knowledgeable.

Abbot) I am going to try. But do allow me to refreshen, once again, the idea of your vehicle on Life's Boulevard driven by your nous. Now, the cab of your car, where the operator/nous sits, is your heart. The physical heart is where the nous is found, even though it is spirit and not restricted by any perimeter of any sort. So, this nous is three distinct parts which should be in unison. These three parts are the *intelligent*, the *appetitive* and the *incensive*. In order for the nous or mind to work properly, its parts must be in agreement, as we have pointed out. Yet, this, for most of us right now, is far from being the ideal kind of a mindset, because we are ill and cannot help but serve two masters...

141

Pilgrim) Please do continue, Father.

Abbot) The Incensive aspect or Volition is our willpower, and it manifests in our head as anger. We must give it meekness and the love for good works. The Appetitive aspect which desires things must be cultivated by temperance, always. Then the Intelligence can drive us home in one piece without the influence of the wickedness of the passions spitting out blasphemies, playing hard rock and carrying on about being too hot, so to have us roll down the window. The monkeys are waiting to jump in. Do you follow?

Pilgrim) Your words are loud and clear. But if I may ask: where does prayer of the heart fit in all this?

Abbot) I am coming to it. So, for the Volition and Desire, the passionate aspects of the nous to start mellowing out, the Intelligence must be escorted by prayer, at all times. The Jesus Prayer, because of the Holy Name of our Lord and Savior, has tremendous power. Then, in time and with some ascesis/temperance, and by the grace of God, the incensive part of the mind starts disliking sin and that of the Appetite starts craving the desire to know Him better and to hear the prayer being recited. Oh my... when our Desire acquires a taste for prayer then the Cognitive faculty must comply, and the prayer becomes unceasing. Meanwhile, the incensive aspect stokes the fire of prayer lit in one's heart, and with the power of will it possesses, and with anger, chases away the enemy.

Pilgrim) As I recall, you said earlier this afternoon that the nous has the power to stop a bad thought from taking hold of us; something to that effect.

Abbot) Well, now you know how this is accomplished. I have to add, my dear fellows, that what I have briefly described is the twists and turns of a road which leads to dispassion, but this road is not strewn with the petals of a rose bush but with its thorns. However, the adversity afforded those who travel this road promotes mental health and feelings of hope and the love for God. And now to complete our discussion, I offer you a challenge: to find a bit of time in the morning and in the evening and so to breathe in the prayer.

Pilgrim) Oh, excuse me. We have read about this. I speak for all of us, that it gives us great pleasure to hear you speak of it.

Abbot) Yes. I thought you might have read of the breathing technique used to guide the Jesus Prayer inside the chest cavity. But the challenge I offered you is to seek and make time, for methods will not work unless you sacrifice time. If, at intervals throughout the day, you stop what you are doing and you follow my directions and have a father confessor to reveal any sins and shortcomings, then prayer of the heart may come of age before you have completely cleansed your heart of all iniquity. This is all about what you want... On the other hand, if you dismiss the chance of finding something higher, then, what can I say?

Pilgrim) Are you saying that we can find prayer quickly? Really! Could the Desire have such an impact?

Abbot) Yes. If you would be successful in any endeavor, you must want it bad enough and you will think about it. Then you must make an earnest attempt to bring about good results. Now when the noetic prayer "rides" the air inhaled and fills the lungs, the heart is affected in a positive way. You can breathe in and let the Jesus Prayer follow the air down the breathing canal until it finally stops. There where the breath stops, is the heart. Stay there momentarily and then exhale.

Pilgrim) Father, I saw a program where a monk said not to do this. He was pretty serious about it and adamant, for some unknown reason.

Abbot) I understand. He is saying that the Saints are outdated. Do you know that this is why the world is coming to an end? We have this general tendency now to drift away from the old ways into non-traditional non-Orthodox practices. God help us. Why should you pray like St. Gregory Palamas or St. Nicodemos? Put away the Philokalia. Don't say the Jesus Prayer. Just be a good person, go to Church, receive. And do not read too much, don't pray with your heart. These things are not for you.

Pilgrim) We don't agree with these statements. We, as a group, are adhering to the belief that noetic prayer is for everyone. The Saints you have mentioned made this clear for us a long time ago, and now we search the Fathers, we have found a traditional shepherd who guides us, and we go on pilgrimages to learn.

Abbot) This is jolly good. My boys, listen to me: you are not going to find sanctity on the computer. On the contrary. Go to monasteries, where the monks and nuns work out in the fields. This should be your YouTube. Prayer is found within a wrinkled cassock, not before a screen. With dirt on the hands and muddy boots, and with tears and supplications before the Lord and the all-holy Theotokos does a traditional monk find God, and you can also. If laptops gave prayer we would have God-bearing Fathers walking the streets. But this is far from the reality of tradition and Orthodox practice.

Pilgrim) A hermit told me once that to find anything by way of mystical prayer, I must live in the mode according to nature.

Abbot) This is absolutely true. A man cannot go to live in the forest, in a skete, or in a hermitage and bring his I-phone along. He simply will not stay there. He must live like God intended for him to live. By eating wholesome foods, by reading from real books, by working manually, and by

144

praying One-on-one with the One who brought him to being. This hermit-monk has his act together. But you can also profit from this same simplicity. As you sit in your prayer room breathe in the Jesus Prayer and let it join the air inhaled. Forget your emails at this time. Do not worry: the car is locked, your family is asleep, the cat will not die of hunger.

Pilgrim) So first oral prayer and subsequently heartfelt. Is that right?

Abbot) Of course. Most of the Saints of the twentieth century agree that if the prayer joins the breath, it becomes automatic because the breath is automatic. The lungs work always pulling the air and pushing it out. So, one stands there and marvels as they hear the Jesus Prayer being recited rhythmically with each inhalation: Lord Jesus Christ... have mercy on me. And when a person feels the love and the longing of being with their Savior - after several stages of trials and temptations - the heart picks up the name of God and repeats it on its own, whether asleep or awake.

Pilgrim) What other ways can we try to have prayer integrate, to become our own?

Abbot) Have a prayer rope in your hand when you pray. That should eliminate some of the distractions. At home or in church. Say the Jesus Prayer during all the services and the Divine Liturgy. At all times. And have nothing in your pocket when you pray, especially in Church. Put those gadgets away. You can do it.

Pilgrim) We thank you, Father, for your words of wisdom... We will try to do what you say. Please give us your blessing before we depart.

Abbot) May the Lord bless you, my children, and bring you home in good spiritual and physical health. And pray for me the sinner, and for my brothers.

Q) Please Mister... could you tell us about God?

A) God is infinite. He is immense. He is a vast entity who contains within Him all of creation from the billions of Galaxies to the suns, stars, the earth and all therein, down to the bugs and the smallest particles of matter.

Q) How do we know this?

A) Through faith and His revelation in the Old and the New Testaments. God has spoken through the prophets and the Saints in His Church.

Q) What is the Church?

A) The Orthodox Church, which is the Kingdom of God on earth established at Holy Pentecost. It is comprised of all the faithful - the living and those who have reposed throughout the ages.

Q) Can you tell us more?

A) As any Kingdom has subjects, so does our Church have the faithful as subjects. And there is a ruler, Lord Jesus Christ as King, who has total authority and rules over His people with a righteous and mighty hand.

Q) Who is Jesus, really?

A) God incarnate. He is the second Person of the Holy Trinity who took human form and thus became the God-man.

Q) Can you explain?

A) God is three Persons: the Father, the Word and the Holy Spirit. So, the Word took on human flesh and being conceived in the womb of the Most Holy Theotokos, he was born as a man and was given the name Jesus. Jesus was God and man together.

Q) So, he had two natures. Isn't it so?

146

A) Correct. Jesus had a human nature as we all do. He looked, lived and acted like a man but He was also God the Word by whom was created the entire Universe.

Q) Why did God become a man?

A) It is written in Holy Scripture that no one can see God and live. God is and will remain a mystery. We will never know of His essence. God has this fervent desire for us all to be saved. Therefore, He appeared as Jesus and walked the earth He had built. And He taught us Himself what to do to be saved.

Q) what do you mean by "saved"?

A) God is concerned about our salvation. He wants all of us to be with Him for all eternity and not to be condemned in Hell. We have to do the right thing. We have to care about others. Period.

Q) Is that His message to us?

A) Of course. The golden rule is "Do unto others as you would like them to do unto you." It's simple. Not only will we enjoy the afterlife but also we will live well on this earth when we show such conduct toward others. And our conscience will be at rest.

Q) What is a conscience?

A) The voice of God. All people have a conscience regardless of race or religion. If we pay attention we will see that our conscience disapproves when we do something wrong. This sense of doing wrong will not leave us at peace. Whereas a peaceful conscience can be a source of joy.

Q) When we have done wrong what can we do to make it right?

A) Repentance is the key to a clear conscience. We repent, ask forgiveness and also go to confession, which is one of the seven sacraments of our Church. Confession is done before an Orthodox priest.

Q) Why is confession important?

A) To be reconciled with God. Especially if we are to receive Holy communion. We must not approach the Holy Chalice unprepared, with hostility toward others, or sins of the flesh, or when we judge people.

Q) What do you mean by sins of the flesh?

A) Our priest will explain it all to you. We must remember that we think, walk and talk before a God who knows everything. So, we must not be ashamed to confess properly. That is to admit to our faults by not hiding anything at all.

Q) God knows everything?

A) He knows our thoughts; we cannot fool Him. And he knows our past. He also knows what is happening right now to all of us and what we are about to think or do in the future.

Q) So, God knows the future?

A) Exactly. God is All-Seeing. He knew before the world was created, that we would be here together on this day at this hour, who would be in our group, their names, thoughts, needs, desires, talents, and shortcomings. He knew with precise accuracy the content and outcome of our discussion and even what we will eat later for lunch.

Q) Amazing isn't it?

A) Truly. God knows, but then He doesn't predestine. God respects our freedom, and He won't suppress our desires but let us do whatever we want. He just knows the outcome of our actions. All men are free to choose what to do.

Q) Why is that?

A) Because a man is free and rational. He is not an animal which is bound by instincts set by its Creator. Man has freedom to do whatever. He is made in God's image. But let it be clear that there are rules for man which he must follow.

Q) Such as?

A) Well, there are the rules of necessity where he will be punished if he breaks a certain law and thus he is restrained from breaking it. It is also necessary that he must act properly so that he will be accepted in society - we all must. Then, he thinks twice before messing with someone stronger. And there is also the golden rule.

Q) You talked about that earlier. Is it the "Do unto others... ?"

A) Yes. There are penalties when we do not abide by this rule. Society in general cannot function properly when this rule is not set in motion in our everyday dealings with people. And spiritually there is chaos when the guidelines of this rule are not met.

Q) Could you tell us why?

A) As there are mechanical laws and physical laws and natural laws, there are also spiritual laws pertaining to the human soul. When these spiritual laws are not kept, grave are the consequences.

Q) Oh my! Is this true?

A) As true as the day is long. In the Gospel of St. John chapter 1:9, it speaks of the Light which illumines every man who comes into the world. This Light is God the Word who gave us the law of God.

Q) The Ten Commandments, right?

A) Moses' Ten Commandments help our soul to be in agreement with the law of God which is inscribed onto our hearts since our birth. We know what is right and wrong. Every man who lives on planet Earth knows what is good and what is bad.

Q) Then, why do we commit sin if we have this law inside of us?

A) St. Paul in Romans 7:25 says that with the mind he serves the Law of God but with the flesh the law of sin. Our mind is in harmony with the Law of God, but our flesh is ornery. And in ancient times sin abounded until our Lord came and put a stop to it.

Q) But is there a concrete method to be able to be victorious over sin?

A) There is. God the Word who is the Wisdom of God became man and showed us what to do to be in control of ourselves. By praying, fasting, going to church, abstaining from evil deeds etc.

Q) What else?

A) What we need most of all to be, as you say, victorious over sin, is to have the grace of God.

Q) How do we attain the attain the grace of God?

A) We draw onto ourselves the grace of God by living like Jesus. Everyone knows how to do that. Mostly, we have to be compassionate toward others. And we must be enemies of sin and of all evil.

Q) But how can we live like Jesus in the world?

A) The ability to conquer evil is inside of us as is God's law and as mentioned we should strive to live before the presence of God with a clear conscience. Then, with confession and some guidance we move forward, with baby steps at first. Little-by-little we invigorate our innate desire to be like Jesus.

Q) Please, could you continue?

A) We have great potential. When one's longing to imitate Jesus comes to fruition, a sense of joy - not of this world - envelops his entire being and he understands empirically the words: "Learn from me that I am meek and lowly of heart and find rest in your souls?"

Q) Is this for real?

A) This is a fact attested by holy people the world over. Monks (and nuns) who live in Christ-like simplicity are role models for those who seek perfection. They are the proof that the Holy Spirit works in the church.

Q) How about the world? Are there any holy people in cities?

A) Sure, there are. Those who are meek and who love a simple existence. When someone likes to always go to the movies, to play video games, to socialize on the internet, another words, when he is restless, that shows that he does not have joy in his heart. The same when he is a materialist.

Q) A materialist?

A) That is someone who finds happiness in material possessions. To own a big house, a nice car, expansive clothes, things like that.

Q) What is wrong with those things?

A) Happiness comes from within a person when his heart is not attached to material things. It is nice to have them as it is good to have money also so that a man can raise a family, but things cannot fulfill him completely.

Q) What do material things have to do with our battle against evil?

A) A whole lot. Attachment slowly becomes an addiction. When this happens, a person does not have time for parents, siblings, and especially for God. He will spend his free time with his addiction. And knowing that he is addicted so that his precious freedom is restricted, he starts to feel terrible.

Q) Why would he feel terrible doing something that he likes? What does freedom have to do with it?

A) God is freedom and peace. If we don't give Him some of our time He withdraws from us, leaving us empty. What I am trying to say is that we are dependent on God. If we don't pray the grace of God leaves and we feel lost.

151

Q) Could you tell us more about this?

A) This awful feeling starts when a man recognizes that he is addicted. The knowledge he has of the fact that his freedom is lost is coupled with pangs of conscience; that is, he is reproached by his conscience severely. God is talking to him.

Q) What is God saying?

A) He is saying that He wants more quality time. God wants His child to draw closer to Him with prayer. God wants devotion from us, not that he needs it, prayer is for our own good.

Q) You mentioned a joy which is not of this world. Could you explain this?

A) Again, this joy comes from imitating Jesus our Lord. We are created in His image, body and soul. Thus, He is the prototype. When we become like Him and act like Him, we kind of feel good.

Q) Why is that?

A) Now we go back to freedom and self-control. Jesus sets us free from the bonds of addictions, habits, passions... And then we are in control of our own destiny. This must be the greatest of joys.

Q) What are passions?

A) Passions are bad desires that are hard to control. Such as smoking, drinking, gambling. Also anger, greed, envy. There are quite a lot of passions.

Q) Where do passions come from?

A) A passion is a spiritual disease. From a bad habit it turns into an obsession like a strong mania where, when it comes to mind, it must be carried out by him who is afflicted by it. Usually, the tempter is behind it all.

Q) Who is the tempter?

A) The devil. When we don't have God in our life, he steps in and becomes our advisor - God forbid. Then there is trouble with alcohol, drugs, lust, anger, hate, jealousy, what have you.

Q) What sort of thing is this devil?

A) The devils or demons are dark fallen angels who are full of malice toward human beings. They work behind the scenes in quarrels, divorces, crimes, murders and all other evil acts. They provoke all the passions intensely. With hatred, do they operate.

Q) But why?

A) Because of envy. They were once bright angels who are now destined to burn in Hell eternally. They are aware of the love our Creator bestows on humanity, and they do not like it.

Q) Should we fear them?

A) What do you think? Actually, with the advent of our Lord Jesus Christ on earth and the establishment of His Church, their power has been annihilated.

Q) But aren't they still able to do us harm?

A) No one can touch a faithful member of the Orthodox Church. Christ our King will crush him. Unfortunately, many of our fellow men who stubbornly resist God's calling to follow Him have given rights to the evil one and they will pay the price.

Q) Isn't it sad that God does not help them?

A) As we have discussed, God is infinite. His Spirit permeates all matter and fills the whole created universe. God is amazingly powerful. What's more he communicates - in his own way - with you who are here and at the same time with another seven billion people. But... He gave us the freedom to choose.

Q) To choose?

153

A) Yes. He knocks on everyone's door at some point and waits patiently for them to answer. He respects our freedom. We have the right to self-rule, and He will not violate this right.

Q) What did you say about the other Seven billion people?

A) Everyone is made in God's image, and God reaches out to all of them, administering to and advising them. He is not restricted by distance and time or language or the diversity of a culture of certain peoples or the great number of them.

Q But how does God do this?

A) God has an open line with everyone. He imparts information to all and talks to them through the voice of their conscience. It is really incredible.

Q) And you said at the same time?

A) God talks, advises, censures, warns all men and cares for all the other creatures of this earth simultaneously, and also all of nature.

Q) I have heard some say that God is not active in the world now, but He rests. Is this not true?

A) Those who spread such rumors are heretics. God gives life to the plants and everything that crawls, walks, flies and swims, and moves the earth to bring about the four seasons with their various weather conditions. Meanwhile He directs the movement of all the other planets and the stars which adorn the heavens, with clockwork precision.

Q) What about Mother Nature?

A) There is no such thing as Mother Nature. This idea is outdated as far as we're concerned.

Q) When God the Word was among us in the person of Jesus, who cared for the universe? Only the Father and the Holy Spirit?

A) It is written in the Akathist: "Wholly present was the Word among those here below, yet in no way absent from those on high." Even while Jesus was dead and buried, God the Word was always with the Father and the Holy Spirit. The Holy Trinity is indivisible.

Q) Now, about the heretics. If God speaks to every man by his conscience why are there so many different faiths and so many religions?

A) There is also a so-called evil conscience which perverts and distorts the truth. This evil conscience is the voice of the demons. These things don't want love and unity. Their leader, Lucifer, is the father of lies. He wants to take us all to hell.

Q) Could you be more clear?

A) These dark angels' spirits are akin to our spirit. They draw close to us when we are not careful and speak trash. They have a mind as we do, and they hate us.

Q) Could you please continue?

A) In the Orthodox Church a man is safe. These, our enemies, will do all they can to break our Church and have us join other sects, or religions, or even cults.

Q) What can we do to be even safer?

A) Compassion toward your fellow man, as we have mentioned, a frank Confession before an Orthodox priest is very important, love and obedience toward your parents, and fasting.

Q) Why do we fast?

A) The main reason for fasting is to honor Wednesdays and Fridays when our Lord was captured and crucified. And there are other reasons.

Q) What might they be?

A) Our enemy, the tempter, has the power of persuasion. We need willpower to reject an evil thought which he brings to us, and we need to do it fast, lest we fall into temptation as happened to Eve in Paradise. Well, fasting fortifies our willpower.

Q) How is that possible?

A) Whenever we say "no" to something that we like, we strengthen our willpower. This power is God-given so we may use it to fight against sin. But there is yet another reason why we fast.

Q) Such as?

A) When we abstain from a certain rich food, like cake meat, chicken, fish, ice cream, fatty or fried food, or very sweet pastries or pies, we don't have the warfare of the flesh which follows afterwards.

Q) Why is this?

A) Sinful temptations usually appear in our imagination to lure us into committing sin. So, when we eat rich foods or when we fill our belly, straightaway our imagination is stirred, and it starts producing images. And since our stomachs are full, we become sluggish and lazy instead of warding off these temptations.

Q) But can't we have some enjoyment?

A) God has made everything good, and we are allowed to enjoy it but as St. Paul writes: "not everything is beneficial." It is excellent though, to have a good measure in everything as the ancients believed.

Q) What is that good measure?

A) The Orthodox Church gives the good measure and wisely forbids some foods and some acts on certain days to help its members with the problem of over-indulgence.

Q) Forgive me but... why is this a problem?

A) We are beings of habit and get easily addicted to things. Addictions bring illnesses, divorces, accidents, quarrels, crimes and through these evils, faithlessness and alienation from God.

Q) Can we fall so easily?

A) Of course we can. That is why temperance helps us so very much. The simplicity once talked about helps us even more to strengthen our temperance, to find that good measure.

Q) Can a man like a monk who seeks to live simply truly find happiness?

A) Yes, this is the outcome of our struggle in Christ, in His Church. A man with few possessions and desires lives in Paradise always, whether he has a car, money or not. And with the sacraments, prayer, and love for all men, then slowly he can come into dispassion. This is the work of the Church.

Q) Is he then perfect?

A) You got it! St. Seraphim of Sarov talked about the acquisition of the Holy Spirit. A dispassioned man has reached sanctity. He is a product of the Holy Spirit. But one who has attachments and bad habits is miserable wherever he is, and whatever he does.

Q) Could you tell us more about temperance?

A) Earlier, we had made reference to the flesh being ornery or rebellious, let us put it this way. Now, the soul wants God, longs to know and to serve Him, and finds peace in the church, but the body doesn't want to be here. So, after our discussions we have arrived at this point where we see more clearly the way of the Holy Fathers, their reason for battling against sin, and the end result which is holiness.

Q) So, the Church is a hospital which makes us well?

A) In the Orthodox Church we are healed and saved from perdition. It's made of two parts: the Church Militant and the

Church Triumphant. The Church Militant is comprised of us on earth and the Church Triumphant of those in heaven.

Q) I didn't know that. Can you add any more to this?

A) We are all of one body in the True Church and by the grace of God, in the end, we will be with him our Lord Jesus Christ who is the wisdom and the power of God. He supports us through our daily struggles.

Q) How can we know if we are struggling the right way?

A) By having a spiritual father. He will show us how to be vigilant, prayerful, and wise to the ways of the Lord.

Q) Thank you so much. Can you please pray for us?

A) Through the prayers of our holy fathers, Lord Jesus Christ our God, have mercy upon us and save us. Amen.

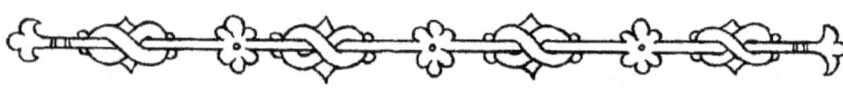

Spiritual Tips

- *When asleep the nous is totally in the heart.*
- *When we wake, a portion of this spirit, which is in the heart, fills the head.*
- *When this portion of the nous fills the head, the brain begins to work, along with the imaginative faculty, and we start to think.*
- *To stop imagination, remove some of the spirit of nous (the focus) from the head.*

THE NOUS, PART 3

... confidence. Yet, this idea of descending with the nous to the heart, to put the nous to the heart, is almost too easy to be true. Yes, this is a fact. Because by "nous" the Fathers do not mean the Intellect, the thoughts, or brains or some other incredible thing but their attention. For the nous is also defined as "attention". This definition solves the enigma of the descend, or the return of the nous to the heart. The "nous energy" coming out of the "nous essence" at the heart, is the subtlest attention without which the brain cannot funtion. But this definition also includes focus, awareness, consciousness. All these are nous in affiliation as the "subtlest attention" which rises to head-level from the heart along with ideas, concepts, thoughts, so to help our cerebral faculties in their work. When we are not attentive thoughts vanish—another words. Where the attention, awareness, focus goes, there goes the nous. No one can certainly move his Intellect hither...

Continued on page 209

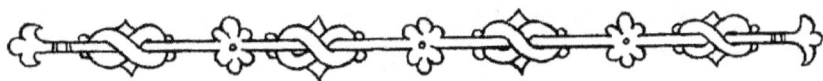

THE DIALOGUES, PART 3

A DIALOGUE WITH A MONK ABOUT NOETIC PRAYER - THIRD TALK

Q) Tell us, Father, why all this ascesis of the Saints?

A) The devils go to the idle and lazy who live in luxury. Discomfort drives them away. This is a mystery for most people. The evil spirits feed on the pleasures of the flesh. That's their ice cream. Especially in western societies where to feel good is "in" and happiness is the highest pursuit, adversity is "out": we hate and avoid it at all costs. That's why man is depressed, and in and out of psychiatric clinics. The pursuit of worldly happiness can never satisfy our souls and, in fact, can leave us deeply empty. The early saints had a different style.

Q) So, should we not look for any pleasure in prayer?

A) Pleasure abounds in prayer but it is of a different kind. Modern folk think of pleasure as a thrill, full of intensity. They have done everything; they have tried it all and nothing is new and exciting to them. When you speak of peace and love they look at you as being an oddball. They want a quick shot o' juice, to be electrified!

Q) How do we turn it around to get on the right track and be healthy?

A) Do not look for pleasure. I remember a while back when I asked an "old-school" cousin of mine, "Do you find some peace in life?" And he replied: "I haven't thought about it." In the old days you would almost never hear people speaking of peace, it was a given.

Q) Weren't they ever troubled?

A) Trouble is common to all, but why bring it up? Thinking about it is not going to help. So, by the same token, do not think of a good time when you pray. It will come when you least expect it. I would say you should not even want it.

Q) These things you say are new to us. Is the stillness then something we would want?

A) Good question. It seems that you are apprehending the fact that you cannot yet handle the stillness which the Holy Fathers speak of. You are in a different mode now. Hesychia is barren of any stimulation of the kind you are used to. This is a start. Now that you understand this, try to convert and slowly, little by little, you may come to fully appreciate the emptiness which hesychasm provides. To be empty of everything except God, for even just a short while.

Q) I have felt this. It is really a wonderful feeling. How do I get it back?

A) I know. I sound like a broken record but here we go again: simplicity, patience, temperance, purity. A man can have ten children and still have a pure mind. Who among you does not get this?

Q) Is pure prayer for the pure mind?

A) They make a great couple. But there is some hope for everyone who is interested. After all, no one is perfect. We are all "in the soup." Find some time to try hesychia as medicine. When your nous picks up the Jesus Prayer life will change. Do not underestimate the value of the prayer in the heart. You will be amazed at the outcome when all is said and done.

Q) You make the application of this prayer easy. Could you give us a clue as to why?

A) The answer lies in the terminology. A nous is all our thoughts, impulses, urges, whims, memories... Nous is also cognition.

161

So, a nous thinks, feels and recognizes noetic concepts. And the nous is contained in our heart. It uses the brain to intellectualize, to rationally come into conclusions, to solve problems, and to create ideas. So, our intellect, that "wise guy," is in the head being the fruit of reason and the nous in English translations is thought of and defined as such. This is why there is so much confusion...

Q) Please continue?

A) The nous, as I have often repeated, is our faculty of thought and it can also be defined as awareness, attention, or focus (definitions for Greek everyday use) by which the mystery of the prayer of the heart is solved. This prayer calls for the descent of our nous/awareness down into our chest, NOT for our intellectual upbringings, our mindful chatter, or the concepts we design and fashion by our brains.

Q) So, nous is not intellect?

A) The intellect is an offspring of our intelligence, but the nous is the content of our heart, and it has consciousness, being like a guard on duty. It is aware of itself, and attentive of everything physical and spiritual. It senses a certain spot by virtue of its focus, which sends signals back to the nous to supply information and get feedback as to where it might go next. The nous is boss. By the awareness, and attention, up at our head, it works on the computer, the brain, and gets information.

Q) We see. So, our awareness is also called nous, right? And nous is also our focus?

A) Yes. And this nous we guide to where we want by sensation. When we inhale, where our breath stops, we make that our focal point. The nous, our awareness, gathers itself there at that place, or anywhere on our bodies, at will, to be conscious of that spot, to be aware where it is now located, to be

162

attentive and focused. So, we bring the focus down into our chest and that is how the union of nous and heart is achieved.

Q) Could you give us a sample to go by?

A) Of course. Please listen. Take the thumb and forefinger of your right hand and give a good pinch to your left arm. Now let go. Do you feel that? Yes? Well, now your nous, your attention, that is, is there. If that feeling was at your heart, your nous would be there instead.

Q) And you say the nous has consciousness?

A) The consciousness, and the other three qualities I mentioned, give an idea of the characteristics attributed to the nous. So, the nous is alive and conscious. If the scholar-translators of ascetical literature keep these four terms in mind, they would understand aplenty and would translate correctly. And so, I think that intellect or mind can somewhat refer to nous, but for the purpose intended, we must think of the nous as "awareness."

Q) Does it not make sense that we cannot return our intellect to the heart?

A) Do you see it now? This is the problem when the nous is defined as intellect, and then no one understands what is going on. When we think of the nous as being focus, it is possible to apply the method of "returning the nous back to the heart." Otherwise, this saying remains incomprehensible. Now, in the beginning, we could face difficulties with attention and focus but as we practice and we do what the teacher tells us to do, our nous becomes strong and agile and quickly focuses and moves about with great speed. In time we become more sensitive, and our nous finds the heart easily and attaches there. When this happens, the whole thinking operation is brought to a halt.

Q) You said that we think as we imagine. Correct?

163

A) We think with images and the devil fights us by using images. In order to fight back we must disrupt our thinking process. To disrupt our thinking process, we must eliminate the fantasy. And we do this by noetic prayer whereby our nous/awareness falls safely down into our chest. Imagination then stops.

Q) Are we still able to think after we put our nous in our heart?

A) When our nous is tucked in there, we are still conscious and we think, but we think simply. Our prayer is turned from cerebral into heart-felt prayer, distinguished by emotion; we pray with feeling and with a loving disposition toward God to Whom we owe our very existence and without Whom life has no meaning. At this time, there is no need for complex intellectual activity or many fancy words. When we love someone, the heart speaks.

Q) And do we pray with any sort of contemplations, intentions, or remembrances, like other traditions?

A) No. Definitely not. When we contemplate spiritually, our subconscious could fall prey to perceiving evil thoughts in disguise as being good. One must be a master to be able to discern which is which. It is dangerous to play with contemplations.

Q) What do you mean? And what is the subconscious?

A) By our subconscious I mean the heart. The heart is the gateway that the spirits come in, whether the good or dark spirits. There is the physical world with which we come in contact using our five senses: the world we know. And there is a parallel world, the spiritual world, which we cannot see but which we feel with our spiritual hearts, which then imparts the feeling to our physical organ, the heart. So, by feeling our fleshy heart, we know sometimes, though not exactly, what is going on spiritually.

Q Could you comment further about the spiritual world and the heart?

A) It is absolutely forbidden to trespass to the other world beyond the limits of our sense perception. It is a spiritual minefield. As far as you are shielded by God and by your common sense and the few poor words of mine, you should be ok. We are immersed in this spiritual world which we cannot perceive. The demons are closer to us than we can imagine. They are at the surface of our heart talking trash to get us to sin. The Lord warned us that the things which defile us come from out of the heart...

Q) Could you please continue?

A) Evil thoughts, therefore, are inspired by demons without our knowledge or consent. The nous which lies in the heart "hears" these thoughts which, by the way, carry an idea in disguise. The nous then, by its reasoning, evaluates and makes a decision as to what to do. The aspect of the soul called *desire*, meanwhile, enters the scene and if it likes what has been presented to the soul, it exerts pressure on the nous to go ahead and to accept the idea.

Q) Is that why we must not have too many desires?

A) That's right. A desire is like a leash. If the nous stands its ground patiently, a man can break free. But his willpower must help the nous to stay firmly fastened to its decision. These three powers *desire, cognition,* and *volition* must be in league for the mind to be healthy and strong. The job, then, of the Orthodox Church is to help them unite.

Q) Is this why the world is in disarray?

A) Man, today, does not know what he is saying. He does not mean what he says, nor does he believe in it. Furthermore, he does not want to say what he means and spreads around what he knows to be lies. He does what he wants not to do. This

165

world has become a spectacle. Because the devils are coming in through the heart unhindered, men will twist a fraud and present it as genuine. And of course, they may or may not believe it themselves, but they will post it to give it credibility, or maybe they will even write a book.

Q) So, the Prayer guards the heart?

A) Yes, the Jesus Prayer contains the Name of God and it is powerful! But, as an aside, let me also mention that the reason we cannot feel the life-giving and awesome power of the Prayer is because we expect a different feeling than what it provides. When modern man prays, he wants to feel good and excited, that is what he knows. We are accustomed to the frenetic and exciting feel of demonic energy, and we are completely desensitized to the calm, peaceful feeling of divine energy. We cannot even feel or recognize it. This is why many people seek overcharged emotional church experiences which make them say: "I got some grace today." But who knows what that experience truly was? At any rate, I can show you some ways to put the cork on the bottle, to block the evil thoughts. Would you like that?

Q) Could you please, Father? We're all ears.

A) Oh! And, before I go on, there is something I must stress: when you guys go back home, and you want to pray noetically, first go to see your priest to pass it through and get it "stamped." You are all healthy mentally, but there are a few out there who are too sensitive and who see ghosts and apparitions, who believe in dreams and in such things. Even if one prays with regular book prayers it is still advisable to let one's confessor know what he or she is doing. And, as we discussed before, humility is a crucial factor in spiritual growth; therefore, we never do things "in the dark" or of our own accord, we ensure that we have our priest's blessing in our endeavors.

Q) So, God can approve?

A) Yes. And now try this: breathe in gently and pause. Where your breath stops, stay there for a bit and, inside you, say the Jesus Prayer a few times. Let's do it together... Breathe in, stop, say the prayer a few times with your inner voice. Now breathe out. And now let us do it again. When you do this a few times, gently as I've said, the cavity in your chest will slightly expand and you are most likely to feel as if your nous has entered therein along with the air.

Q) Where have I read this?

A) Possibly in the first letter in *Monastic Wisdom*, that great book. So, when you finally have safely enclosed your nous within and you are aware of the boundaries of this cavity, then let the nous adhere itself there by the sensation it possesses. Do not let the nous come out of this space with the air as you exhale but trap it as in a jail. Success or failure depends on finding the hole, this space, bringing your awareness inside and saying the prayer there with the voice of the heart.

Q) I am able to put my nous inside of me, but it won't stay for long. What can I do?

A) First off, remember your humility: you are not a monk. Start with small goals. Ten to twenty seconds at a time is a real accomplishment for a layman. Most importantly: do not judge. You are smart people and smart people tend to judge others, but judgement works against you. Remember that judgmental thoughts which come into the heart and rise to the head, they are not yours. So, if they are not yours, why bother listening to them? Turn the channel to another station and keep doing that as many times as needed.

Q) I want to ask something. At what point can we stop evil thoughts? If it's possible to do so.

A) Once again, thoughts flood the place of the heart, always trying to come in. The nous then perceives one of the many prowling thoughts and, by the power of reason, lying in the head, analyzes it and prepares to reject or accept the offer the thought has presented. All thoughts are fueled by an idea offered to us for examination and approval. After a particular thought ends, another begins. Let me tell you something: you cannot stop thoughts simply by the force of your own will.

Q) So, Father, is there anything we can do to stop the thoughts?

A) Do not pay any attention to them, it is all you can do. Actually, you cannot impede the flow of thoughts but nothing can force you to pay attention. Do you get it now? By taking your attention from the head, you accomplish this great achievement. You become deaf to incoming thoughts. The flow of evil conceptions still continues but nobody's home and they go unnoticed. You do not either reject or accept; nothing.

Q) Can I ask? What happened to our first parents? Did their thoughts betray them?

A) In their case, it was different altogether. They did not have evil thoughts assailing them. They were dispassionate and holy with their bodies and souls radiating God's grace. Eve did not converse with the snake inwardly. She saw the snake with her eyes, it was not a vision of some sort, and she spoke to it: this snake was real. But after the fall and the ousting from Paradise all their offspring have the snake fighting them from the inside with notions, thoughts, desires, tendencies, and passions.

Q) Were they distressed or pressured in any way to agree and go along with the snake's proposal?

A) Look, I was not there. But there is overwhelming evidence which leads to the conclusion that we are easily charmed. Demonic energy has such properties. It sensually allures humankind, it fascinates, attracts, and puts "a spell" on the poor fellow who engages in a conversation with an evil thought.

Q) That is certainly true. Do we not all agree?

A) There you have it. Are we in need of more witnesses? My children, listen he has the power of persuasion as his weapon and we are all ill, we are liable to succumb to temptation at any minute, even as we speak. So do not talk to him. Leave him alone.

Q) How far can the devil take it, as far as being able to manipulate us?

A) We learn from the story of Job that he must get permission from God to tempt us. Now, I do not think that you should, tinkering as a fool, try to figure out God's plan. The "whos" and "whys" and "ifs" should be left alone. Try to do what the Saints prescribe. Take a few minutes a day to feel your heart and put the name of Jesus there in close proximity.

Q) This is nice. Are there other ways to stomp the assaults quickly?

A) Another interesting exercise to do, to break up imaginings and things, is to think of the two parts of an hourglass. The top bulb is your head and the bottom of your upper chest. Let the trickling sand be the nous/attention. The sand will soon empty into the chest and so will your attention; keep the head empty and the sand/attention down in the bottom and you will pray undistractedly.

Q) Do you have any more?

A) Our nous is like a magnet attracted to a piece of iron in our head. As soon as we awake – boom! – it goes up to the brain, just like you boys awake and head straight for your electronic screens to revel. Information, education, the news, any and all kinds of intellectual tasks and endeavors appeal to the mind. Because it is made for this work just like an engine is made to propel a vehicle. So, if you care to keep your nous under control when you pray, keep that magnet in your chest and do not let it come up to your head. Simple.

Q) Did you say that the nous is made for intellectual work?

A) The problem is that it does not know when to stop. It gets carried away thinking, and solving, and imagining. It gets addicted and, with the passions working at full speed with the imagination, what comes out of the heart is uncontrollable. Like herds of cattle in a stampede.

Q) You have told us many times about the imagination. How did our Lord think, if I may ask?

A) Our Lord Jesus Christ is called the second Adam. I am not in a position, as a sinful man, to comment on your question but I quote something by Georgios Koresios: "The nous of Christ was completely independent of the imaginations which become a wall blocking the immaterial realities of the spirit." Whatever that means. I remembered the quote, but I have no clue as to how I may come to understand it. They say that Adam did not have imagination either, or Eve.

Q) Is that why our Lord did not imagine the devil during His three temptations, but really saw him?

A) Christ did not imagine him but saw him in plain reality. Our Lord, just like Adam and Eve before the fall, did not do battle with evil thoughts inwardly, as we all do. The saints head back to the primordial state of being, once fantasy is abolished, by the grace of God.

Q) You have explained about fantasy's hold on us. I am kind of scared, why is this thing holding on?

170

A) I cannot put my finger on it but what I am saying comes from my own life's experience, that fantasy mesmerizes a person to a high degree. But in our condition, we can't live without it. Sometimes imagination helps us to resolve problems, to plan or to hope, and these are good things. I would say do not think about it. If you have to daydream for the future, for the welfare of your children, to prepare for a special event, to forget your problems, so be it. But reject such daydreams during prayer.

Q) Can we pray noetically to the Theotokos?

A) I do, when in trouble I seize my inner voice and call on the "Panagia, Panagia, Panagia, Panagia, Panagia." You know what? Nothing moves. The demons go dumb. Try it and you will see this yourself.

Q) I do, with your suggestion, a little bit of the Akathist every day. Is it that strong?

A) The salutation to our sweet Mother must be at the pinnacle of all devotional services. The Theotokos truly saves. Our Geronda told us to do the whole Akathist twice a day and, since then, we push ourselves to learn it by heart. Also, her supplications are good to read. Just to think of the Panagia is life changing. She gives the prayer of the heart, consoles, heals, encourages, sympathizes with us. She comforts and never disappoints.

Q) We see that.

A) Initially you asked me to speak to you about prayer. If all of you want to have success, spiritually, do a little bit of the Akathist, even if only a few lines, daily and you will feel her embrace; you will see miracles. Noetic prayer is connected to the care of the Theotokos. She has a lot of "pull," being our Savior's Mother. Rejoice, O bride unwedded!

Q) She is truly special. Now Father, let me ask, could you go over the breathing technique once again?

A) There are two ways a man can profit by breathing in the prayer. You were introduced to both ways earlier. With the first, we inhale and exhale saying the Jesus Prayer, and by doing so the prayer sticks to the breath, and as the breath is self-acting so the prayer also becomes self-acting, in time. The second way is to pull the nous with the Jesus Prayer through the air canal and into the greater lung area and leave the nous and the prayer in there as we breathe out. Then, we breathe gently in and out while having our nous/focus and the prayer in that crevice throughout.

Q) Does this movement of the air into the lungs serve to help return the nous back to the heart?

A) You know it! Do not forget that when we say nous, we mean the "think tank" in our heart, for one, but also our consciousness/awareness which is also called nous. Let me add that the former relies on the latter to have its thoughts manifested and worked over. For a human being, nous and consciousness are inseparable. And in order to be fully realized, our consciousness needs the active participation of the brain when we are awake and alert.

Q) What if, when praying, we are not totally alert?

A) Do not pray in the heart, when you are not "all there." When the consciousness starts shutting down, imagination begins. When unrestrained imagination flares up, that means that the enemy is entering through the heart without a passport. As I have pointed out, we are immersed in a spiritual energy field filled with demons and the mind must exercise its authority over the logismoi.

Q) So, to be attentive is crucial?

A) We must remain attentive and aware and, when we put our nous to the heart, we have to leave some awareness behind. The head must have enough attention to look out for trouble. Initially, I would say to have 50% nous in the head and 50% in the heart or in the hand, if we are praying with the prayer rope. As we progress in prayer, gradually this ratio will change in favor of the heart or hand.

Q) Can I ask? What is the nous-essence or nous-energy we read about?

A) I did not bring this up so as not to complicate matters. But since you ask, I will answer simply. The essence is the cause of energy. Like a fire: the essence is the flames and the heat being produced is the energy. So, our nous-essence begets thoughts in the heart. These thoughts rise to our head as energy.

Q) Could you tell us more about the consciousness?

A) We are made in God's image. Look at the trees. They have their life's essence down at the roots and energy is rising up their trunk to the branches and leaves. They are alive and nourished by nutrients found in the earth and water. A tree is a whole mechanism, working precisely by the seasons and climate. But a tree is not conscious or aware; it does not have a nous. It does not have free choice either. Even the animals do not have a choice. They are bound by instincts and natural laws pertaining to each kind.

Q) What exactly are you trying to say?

A) I think that our consciousness has to do with our free will. Humans are rational beings and free. For man to sin before the face of God, he must know what he's doing. I am saying that man has something that none of the other creatures have: a quality that makes him very special. So, look, for the nous or mind to rationalize, to devise explanations, and to

173

formulate opinions, it uses its consciousness, the guard and custodian, to open the office and to turn on the "computer," our brain.

Q) Interesting. And then?

A) Then the nous starts up to work on the computer, to program and to analyze and decide. The nous uses the charts and books of experience, discernment, common sense and the know-how it gathered from previous undertakings to get this job done. When the work is completed, the nous files the information obtained from this particular project into memory and stores it away. Now, meanwhile, the guard on duty is looking out for trouble and it has brought its three sons along: the awareness, attention and focus. The four of them help the nous to complete the task at hand.

Q) Wow, it's like a little factory, isn't it?

A) Well, our consciousness has to help the nous: they go together for the operation to work. And if we do not have evil desires to tyrannize us, and if our will power is strong enough to put an end to any brawls and conflicts that arise during our decision-making, then the operation works like a clock.

Q) Father, could you, please, tell us something about the intellect?

A) Oh, the "wise guy." Actually, this prodigy is our foolishness. The intellect is like that baseball cap the nous wears before it sits on the swivel chair in front of our brain's computer. On the front, this cap has the inscription written in large, capitalized letters: "SUPER GENIUS." You understand. Our intelligence is powered by hot air; real wisdom comes from God to His humble servants.

Q) Super genius, huh?

A) The point I am making is that we must not think too highly of our own intelligence nor give it too much room to roam; otherwise, we can reason ourselves into many fallacies and

174

heresies. But when we are focused below the neck and are aware of what the heart is doing, the logic goes out to lunch (laughs). We cannot have our logic around when we pray. For example, when we are in our room trying to gather our minds and we have an uninvited guest in the kitchen drinking our wine and eating out of the fridge, how can we pray? We have to close the windows and doors to our nous, our soul, to be with the Lord. Can't get up in the morning to find a stranger sleeping on the couch. This frequently happens with uninvited thoughts. Because of too much intellectual activity.

Q) Time to regroup. Too much office time, you think?

A) Literally. You guys should be planting. That's right, planting a garden of simplicity out back, after you till it with the hoe of repentance. Then you should walk around the fence of your soul to see if there are any openings which dark jackals might come through to eat your dog. And then check the doors and seal the windows of your senses to prevent a draft of evil propensities slipping through to disturb the peace.

Q) And then?

A) Hum... Visit the elderly, those wholesome reflections that you have neglected. Feed them with Church time and the Jesus Prayer. Pick up a prayer rope, put your nous on the knots. Say the prayer as you listen to the holy words and do it with yearning and love. You know, with a whimper like you are a beggar before Christ. The methods and the techniques I show you will take you to the feet of Jesus our Lord.

Q) I forget this sometimes, why?

A) Remember the great commandment. To love God with all your heart, soul, and mind. I am not telling you to be a monk, the "Great Commandment" is not just for monks. I am saying that if you want prayer as a friend and companion in your life, you must put in effort. If we do anything in life and we want to

175

excel in it, we should have our mind always on it. We should desire it badly enough to strive with all our might to achieve it. It's plain and simple. Remember the great commandment found in the Gospel of Matthew: "You shall love the LORD your God with all your heart, with all your soul, and with all your mind," and remember the three powers of our soul.

Q) What other techniques do you recommend?

A) Before I go on you have to understand that these exercises are not an end to themselves but only help to curb the nous. This is not yoga. Once we help the nous to find stillness our prayer will flow like a murmuring stream. Not for the health of the body but for the health of the soul.

Q) They say in the books to hold one's breath while praying noetically, what do you say about that?

A) Good question. By the way, I need to remind you: if you do not ask you will not learn so, when you try something different be sure to ask first! Ask anybody. Doing things on one's own is self-reliance, which is the opposite of humility. I am telling you of what happens when people get too confident regarding spiritual things: this is stupidity. I mention this now because this idea of holding the breath while saying the prayer must be escorted by discernment and knowledge and requires guidance.

Q) Could you go on?

A) Now that you've asked with humility, I will say this: pause after every inhalation of the Jesus Prayer only two seconds; truly, only two seconds. You have to breathe and repeat the Jesus Prayer gently and lovingly. You are not running frantically on the street to catch the bus. Say the Prayer and pause: easy does it!

Q) I needed to hear this, Father. Now, do I say the whole Prayer once with every breath?

A) You can say half of the prayer breathing in "Lord Jesus Christ," and the other half out "have mercy on me." Or say the whole prayer once when breathing in and the whole breathing out. Or two prayers in and two prayers out, or three. This depends on the capacity and strength of your lungs, and on the rhythm that feels most natural and prayerful to you.

Q) Did you not tell me once about using the nous as a probe during prayer?

A) You have a good memory... Let us suppose we have a cave on the upper half of our torso, right under the neck. Now, our neck is the entrance to this cave. From there we guide a probe slowly down into the cave. I do not remember what I told you exactly, but the probe serves as a good analogy. Our nous is this round, bean-sized probe. Let it wander and move in the cave, to and fro, back and forth, up and down, to get a feeling that it is located within an enclosure.

Q) I see the cave under my neck for some reason. Why is this?

A) When the nous hears a word the imagination right away makes it an image. When we hear the word "house", we imagine a house, when we "hear" horse we "see" a horse, when we hear "steak," we "see" a juicy steak, and our mouth waters.

Q) Is that so?

A) Of course. I deliberately talked of a cave and an enclosure wherein our nous may enter and you instantly caught on, all of you. With an effort you will be able to sustain this feeling so that your nous will be occupied down below in the "cave" of your heart.

Q) But aren't we employing imagination which is a no-no?

A) Initially, some slight form of an image will appear to help us focus on that part of the body where we want the nous to be. Once we bind our focus to that place, we delete from our imagination even that little bit of a picture for our mind to be

177

completely pure. Besides, we cannot avoid a faint image which certainly will appear once we feel a spot.

Q) Should we pray with eyes open, or eyes closed?

A) In the beginning it is good to have your eyes open. Why? Because if the mind is not supplied with a picture of something that exists in reality, it will make one up. The imagination, this troublemaker who upsets people for a living, is always too eager to portray in his paintings the lies and the gossip, the filth, and all the refuse of the passions that is worthless and entirely offensive. The imagination loves our enemy. He is like a double agent who works for us and for the enemy. With time and practice, though, the experienced will scorn this evil and will close their eyes to pray.

Q) You have talked of stillness several times. Could you elaborate?

A) The stillness I refer to is not the eastern-style emptiness these boys in Asia are looking for as they exercise meditation, self-denial, and indifference to life, like the ancient stoics, to bring about what they call "dispassion" and "blessedness."

Q) But isn't dispassion our goal?

A) I think you know what I mean: the dispassion of those people is a mortification of the soul, which is not the same as the Orthodox context. For us as Orthodox Christians, "dispassion" is a sanctification of man and therefore the powers or aspects of his soul are transfigured and are directed toward God. Hesychia or stillness is deliverance from the passions, at last.

Q) I know people who practice stillness. They stand and look out there at nothing. What do you think of that?

A) After the primordial fall, man is prone to idolatry, and toward strange religions, and the unknown. Even Christians fall into the occult. We have visionaries who interpret dreams, who like to prophesy, who call on the spirits, etc., and some are regular church goers! And we have those practitioners who meditate, who look for signs, and who go into a trance for long hours in the dark. I am not talking about going fishing to find some peace. But this type of "stillness" you mentioned is suspect. Stillness done for spiritual revival can inadvertently take on a pantheistic character.

Q) I do believe you. Tell us, how can we find some quiet time?

A) It depends on what you are really after. There is external stillness with a quiet living away from cities, marked by a humble lifestyle. And there is internal quietude influenced by an Orthodox mindset. Those two can easily coexist.

Q) I was asking about interior prayer. How do I start?

A) You must make time to pray! I know, you are super busy: you have to check the weather, read your emails, feed the cat, make breakfast for the kids. You have no time for God, this is the norm for morning rituals these days. At night you crash after dinner, or stay up to play a video game, or go to social media to be with your friends, telling yourself "Go ahead you deserve it..." but later always feeling that you are failing to redeem your time. But you can turn this around, my friends, there is joy in prayer, if you want it. Start tomorrow.

Q) I guess we need a schedule. Is that right?

A) The biggest demon is that of negligence. Without a schedule you are prey for the beasts. We humans are beings of habit and by good habits we are victorious over ourselves. It is not important how much prayer you do as much as when you do it, and at what time. A tight schedule is the answer. And a good night's sleep.

Q) But the Holy Fathers say not to sleep a lot, is that right?

A) Relying on books is not a good thing. Everyone's constitution regarding food, drink and sleep is different. In regard to sleep, the nous/focus, who is guard over the heart, must be well-rested in order to do its job well. You must listen to people with experience in prayer, in order to get prayer.

Q) So, Father, what you are saying is that to have success in prayer we must do whatever you suggest?

A) God is fair. He will give us His grace because He wants to. Let us do our share and be obedient to our teachers. Everyone can find prayer; look at me, I do not have much grace but... even a blind squirrel finds an acorn from time to time.

Q) Father, forgive me. My mind is feeding me bad thoughts about you, telling me you are, well... thoughts I do not want. Why does this happen?

A) I know. Your mind says that I am an idiot. It might be right. Actually, it is your heart saying that. But, as I have said, often our thoughts are not our own. We have an enemy who feeds thoughts to us through the heart, which has an internal voice, and I think I have told you about this.

Q) The inner voice?

A) The inner voice makes known to us what is going on down there on top of the heart where that little voice comes from. Inside the chambers of our heart nothing can enter except the Jesus Prayer. And no one knows what the heart is thinking about but God Himself and sometimes our lowly mind when God allows. It's a deep abyss, the heart. Somewhere close to, or on top of the physical heart, the inner voice or logos is to be found.

Q) Does the devil not know what we are thinking?

A) No. Our logos expresses our heart or transmits what God is saying to us by our conscience, or what we ourselves give it to utter. The devil comes and takes it over sometimes and talks to us, planting thoughts, and we do not really know if it's him or us doing the thinking. But he does not know what exactly we are thinking about; he only knows what he has put in there and what he said himself.

Q) How do the mediums know what a man thinks about and does?

A) The demons know of the thoughts that they themselves have just planted in our noetic garden, not what is safely hidden in our heart. And they know what has transpired in our lives; they keep records. And so, the voice of the tempter we hear noetically, springs from our inner voice. This is the same voice of the snake that talked to Eve.

Q) That same voice?

A) You need an ear-pulling... As if I knew if it was the same demon. The idea is the same and the source is of the same demonic type. So, if we hear something in our head: Boom! We go to confession right away. This is our safety, as I have pointed out. Snakes usually go hiding under a rock. You pick up the rock and they disappear; do you get it? So, sinful or unwelcome thoughts that we hide grow and multiply but those we expose to the light of day dissipate.

Q) I guess we always need to consult God?

A) That is exactly my point, and this is what we do here in the monastery always: consult God by way of the Elder with any such unbidden thoughts. But better yet, we avoid a dialogue with the snake, for prevention. Noetic prayer is prevention, we do not want to have to use prayer to fight a thought we have coupled with: we want to learn to use prayer so that we do not ever even hear that thought.

Q) Isn't this very hard to do, to reject yourself?

A) This is exactly the ideal: to reject a noble upbringing, a sharp cognition, a good education, your looks, high opinions. When thoughts about your abilities, achievements, or anything telling you "You are... something" comes to mind during prayer, this is evil in disguise, most times. It is a great feat for

181

the nous to be stripped of all concepts, ideas, imaginings for a while during our communication with God. It is thus illumined.

Q) To be stripped of everything?

A) Well, to have only love for Jesus, but in a simple form, unadorned by exaggerated expressions or hype. Now, by breathing in the Jesus Prayer the nous becomes accustomed to partially emptying out of the head in order to be pulled down into the chest cavity. And since emotions abound down there (near the heart), the love comes easier.

Q) I have had a problem with my lungs since I was young. What can I do?

A) Do not take deep breaths. As you breath out – try this everybody – let your nous, as if it is the anchor of a ship, slowly drop from your head down into your chest, there. So, you do not have to breathe in the prayer, let it drop down as you breathe out gently. Where the anchor stops there is your inner voice. Now start reciting with this voice the Jesus Prayer.

Q) About self-acting prayer, when will it take place?

A) This will come with time and practice working the Jesus Prayer, orally, at times, or with the voice of the heart, and being patient during your temptations and practicing gratitude for what God has bestowed on you, such as the oxygen you breathe, your health, your life... This is further aided as you take a few minutes every day to do a small piece of the Akathist to the Most Holy Theotokos. With this focus on prayer, you are preparing the ground for the advent of this most wonderful gift; for the heart to say the prayer of its own accord. This is something awesome.

Q) I think that I am starting to understand but please continue.

A) Prayer of the heart is when the heart prays. When a man gets there, he will be in another level of prayer. But, again, there will be trials first, whether trials with others, with temptations, with your passions, or with your life…, for quite a while.

Q) Did you say quite a while?

A) It really depends on you. Are you willing to step on your ego? Then we will see. Can you find the time to sacrifice? Can you take the troubles of life in stride? Spiritual life mirrors the physical. To acquire anything, you must pay. There is a price tag on this prayer: humility. If you are not willing to struggle, the return of the nous to itself will not happen. Oh, I hear the bells for vespers. Let's go to church. I will see you after the service of Small Compline.

Continued on page 231

Spiritual Tips

- *We direct our focus/attention away from our head by using sensation to place focus on another spot on the body (it is best to place this focus somewhere below the neck).*
- *When we feel that spot, the nous/focus goes there. The best is when we feel the heart, and our focus goes there.*
- *The imaginative faculty cannot work when the focus/attention/awareness is not at head.*

Faithful) Tell us, Elder: how can we use the practical advice you give us as a family?

Elder) The family is a Church and so our monastic community is also a family. These two institutions are arenas where the Orthodox struggle to acquire perfection, dispassion that is. We both go against the eight deadly sins but in different settings. We confront them here, and you, at home.

Faithful) I didn't know that. Could you tell us more about this? We do know of these deadly vices.

Elder) Good. So let us go over them and see what we can do to confront them successfully. Now, when a monk sits at the refectory, he does not know what to expect by way of food. He only knows that it is either non-fasting or Lenten, but he will eat it regardless and gives thanks always. And thus, the passion of gluttony is restrained.

Faithful) Oh... I guess we can do the same at home.

Elder) Of course. Do not give the children a choice. Let them eat whatever is there at the table. The same with the spouse - you have to eat what the cook offers - you don't want to offend. If the entry does not satisfy your palate, put some hot sauce on it. And think of places around the world where there is no food to eat, or clean water to drink.

Faithful) My question is: is it sinful to enjoy a meal? After all, God provides for our food.

Elder) Let me explain. If I can have a burger, my bowl of soup will not be adequate. If the children are given a choice, they will not enjoy what is placed before them, because the parents have given the evil one a weapon to fight them with. But without a choice, they will learn to enjoy their meal, and they will be grateful. You see, the quality of thought makes sitting at the table a pleasant experience, not the food.

Faithful) I'm trying to take this in, it is new to me.

Elder) Freedom of choice, my friends, is not evil in itself but it opens doors to new challenges for children, young people, and even grownups. If one gets into a habit of choosing, selecting or preferring to do this over that, this person will not be at peace when feeding the dog or cleaning his room, making the bed, washing the dishes for mom, vacuuming, cutting the grass, since he can choose not to. Why obey US law? Why work for a living? Why stay married if divorce is an option? Is this what kind of a person you, as parents, will give to society? Be careful! A man needs to be disciplined to survive life's battlefield. He or she must be trained to be able to push through when adversity strikes. And it all starts at home, at the table. If our youth are strong enough to abstain from delicacies on a fasting day and can take all food down with a smile, then they can say no to drugs and alcohol, and to bad company. Remember that we are Orthodox, a step ahead of the rest...

Faithful) It all makes a lot of sense. Please continue.

Elder) Well, then gluttony feeds the vice of lust where a person yields to sinful desires. Because by not being able to have control at supper one cannot have control of the carnal passions. The sensual pleasure that derives from consuming savory foodstuffs is the same. So, it transfers to lust and entices the senses to continue to feel this blissfulness, if you will, way after the meal is over. This is the reason we fast before taking Holy Communion, so as not to be provoked. Partaking of rich foods promotes a lively imagination but by fasting a man can take a hold of this faculty and by praying puts it to sleep. So, there is the passion of gluttony and then the passion of lust. These two are a tag team.

Faithful) Hmm, I have never...

Elder) Monks know many things from experience. You never heard or read some of the truths that I am disclosing but there is a time for everything. Start today, you have a monastery at home. You too can have the ideal mindset to combat the evils you face and to attract the grace of God. Now, the next sin in succession is that of greed - money is the root of all evil. One also can be obsessed by the acquisition of material things when money does not exist, like as if in a monastery. A monk has no money, but he can gather in his cell clothing, several pairs of shoes, gadgets, broken rakes, strange tools, clocks that don't work...

Faithful) Like a hoarder?

Elder) Basically. But greediness is somewhat healed because there is no cash. At home then when one gets married greediness is healed since parents must provide for their children. So, God has set family needs as a way to be rid of this passion. Still, in both of these sacred institutions, material things are shared and that helps to keep the love as well as order.

Faithful) So it's not mine, mine, mine, mine anymore. But if I may ask what passion is next?

Elder) The next one on the list is anger. This one is terrible and must be kept under lock and key at all times. Here in the monastery, we have learned, since we were novices, not to confront each other for any reason whatsoever - NONE. Never, never, never, never, never, never... This, the devil wants so much to hurt the ones you love. When you give in and you lose it - do you notice how quickly and easily the words are composed and the speech executed where it seems

186

that it's not you but someone else who is speaking? I don't want to scare you, but I believe this: that when someone is overtaken by wrath/fury, he or she is not themself, but it is the snake who has taken over. It's almost like possession. In that state of mind people commit murder. And they confess afterward: "I did not know what I was doing."

Faithful) Wow! Elder, you struck a chord. Now I understand. When I am mad, I get creative.

Elder) Sure. Words come out clear and very strong. At this time, you can put someone in the hospital because the devil knows what hurts, what words are the most ruthless and damaging. I'm telling you he is the one DOING the talking. It's a pity that most people don't understand, and they let the tongue rule over their reason. They call their own children names, and their spouse, and their household becomes a dwelling place for those inventors of wickedness. When they fight, these things are dancing like crazy. They will instigate domestic violence and cause a divorce.

Faithful) Should we not get angry at all? Is this what you are saying?

Elder) No, one of the powers of our soul is that of Volition/Willpower or the Incensive power as it is called otherwise. This God-given power manifests in a man's mind as anger. It is the strength of spirit that we have to help us achieve a goal, to overcome a problem, to accomplish what we have set out to do. A brew of this anger can help us safeguard our families and give us the fortitude to say no to sin and to ward off the demons. But it is forbidden for an Orthodox Christian to use it against his fellow man, let alone the wife and children.

Faithful) How do we gain our health and stop doing this?

187

Elder) As I have pointed out, you allow your marriage, which is so important to you, to help calm you down when the nerves flare up. Use the love you have for your family to make you meek, if you think that this is what you should do. Use your mind that is, do what monks do. Go for confession, take a walk to let some steam out, talk about it later, control yourself. It would be more blessed yet, to warn the children before they get married that this is coming, and not to lose hope but to pray, make amends, forgive each other. After all, we are all human.

Faithful) What did your abbot say to you before entering into monasticism. Did he warn you?

Elder) It is impossible in this life not to have someone make you upset. This will happen no matter what. As for my holy elder, he told me to say two things when faced with this difficult issue: "forgive me" and "let it be blessed". That is all I could say as a novice and then as a monk, that is all! I had no choice. As I have explained to you, a choice opens up a can of worms, to put it in simple words. Monks are not gullible and weak to have the mouth speak before thinking. We are not going to let the evils ransack this monastery, no way. You do the same as we do. Close your mouth and put Christ to work. Be wise.

Faithful) Hmm. We have plenty to think about when we get home.

Elder) My children, it is not only your composure you will lose but also the grace of God. Not only peace but prayer. Not only your health but your livelihood. Uncontrollable anger does great harm. The next vice, the fifth, is what the fathers have called acedia. This one includes within a strong negligence, listlessness, and depression. And uncontrollable anger will bring them on to stay! What did our Lord say? "Learn of Me; for I am meek" There is no justification, and you know what?

188

When negligence strikes, it will empty out any good you've done that week. When combined with pride, that might bring on judgment and condemnation to top it off. From then on, it could get ugly.

Faithful) So all the vices work together, I assume?

Elder) That is correct. They have the same starting point, which is love of pleasure, which comes from food and lust. The love for wealth/greed and love for power/glory is represented by envy and vainglory. Envy, the sixth vice, has no friends or relatives. In the monastery I treat the brothers here the same, so they don't get jealous of each other, and you also do the same with your children, if you want. Also, you should not talk to a stranger of the other gender when your spouse is present. Why let jealousy spoil a beautiful day? And be careful not to be too intimate with your friends. Envy can afflict friendships as well.

Faithful) I have made that mistake a few times.

Elder) All men have, when you get too familiar with people you have problems. Here in the monastery, we try hard not to open up to others. We have our problems, our thoughts, our goals, our own inclinations and desires, why mix it up? You have to have discernment in sharing good news with your friends also. Why tell someone that you hit the Lotto? Do you think that he or she will surely be happy with that? Think again. Not that they are not nice people, but the tempter fights with us all. Envy is always at the forefront and afflicts nearly everyone.

Faithful) How about vainglory, elder? How do you confront this deadly passion?

Elder) We fight against it by our obedience. When a man does what he is told like a servant, he does not think highly of himself. As I told you a few minutes ago, the love for pleasure

189

is the starting point of all the sins. This is the sensual demonic pleasure. Obedience on the other hand is the fragrance of pleasure divine. The seventh and eighth passions, which are this vainglory and pride, are fueled by demonic pleasure, and since we live in this fallen world and are wearing the flesh, we cannot get away from this type of hype except through obedience. Obedience drives away the demons, they don't like it. And thus, the hype becomes peace, joy in the Lord, and love.

Faithful) We have sometimes this love, the peace, and joy in the Lord. This feeling is delightful.

Elder) There you go. Cultivate this feeling then with prayers, with forgiveness, and patience. Humble yourselves, obey each other, show understanding, overlook the faults of others. This way you may taste a bit of the monastic ideal and you will reach perfection, in time. Go home now and try on my admonitions for size.

Pilgrim) Your blessing Father, we have come to see you. Please tell us something about the spiritual life. We have come a long way.

Father) What can I do for you? What would you like to talk about? Our life here? About prayer? Let me see... Perhaps about ascesis?

Pilgrim) Could you talk to us about the famous "Prayer of the Heart"? This could be a big blessing for us. Tell us something from your experience.

Father) Let us sit outside of the front gate. I have something on this prayer that you would be interested in. Well now... You have to remember that the life of a monk is characterized by simplicity, and this is what you have to work on if you too would like to pray this way.

Pilgrim) Please explain it to us: what do you mean by simplicity?

Father) Here in the monastery we only work; we eat, and sleep. Meanwhile we are praying just about all day. It is a monotonous way of life without the rush, hype, and the excitement of an everyday secular lifestyle. We don't work in an office, we have no choice in trapeza, we eat what is there. Then we sleep four hours, and we get up in the middle of the night to pray for seven to eight hours.

Pilgrim) Do you read from the Holy Fathers and the Lives of the Saints?

Father) Of course, we pray and read in our cells for the first four hours after rising, and the rest of the time we spend in church. But you see, there is no time to play, and no reverie, no entertainment, no radio or television, no internet, or even a phone to look at. Furthermore, we don't watch or hear any news. And thus, the stage is set for a spiritual sort of recreation, one that is devoid of sensual pleasure. Our "good time" is that time in our cells when we feel the presence of God and by extension at all other times.

Pilgrim) This sounds new to us. Is sensual pleasure evil that we must avoid it? And what do you mean by "good time"?

Father) Since the transgression of Adam and Eve, sensuality has come into our lives. When our senses are satiated, our love for God is extinguished. This is most prevalent in the western hedonistic societies. As a monk, therefore, I must curtail sensual delight so that God's presence and love abounds through prayer. So, in prayer I feel good in a spiritual way. But also, I feel content.

Pilgrim) We are never happy anymore. With anything.

Father) And that is why you suffer. Noetic prayer, or what they call Prayer of the Heart, is distinguished by emotion coupled with a sense of gratitude. To pray well, we start there. We give thanks for everything.

Pilgrim) I see. Worldly people are afforded much comfort, and they take it for granted.

Father) Exactly. They don't need God anymore. They have everything. Whereas a monk who doesn't have any source of pleasure coming from without, feels a great consolation and his heart flares up with thanks for the little things like the oxygen he breathes and the water he drinks. And this is that sublime work of the nous in a man's heart that prays unceasingly because he appreciates things. This is the "Prayer of the Heart."

Pilgrim) Hmm. I thought it was something different.

Father) You do not have to "google it" to find where this prayer is - it is built into our system. The prayer of the nous occurs spontaneously when a body lives according to its nature. But with this material variety of expressions that I was referring to, with that addiction and the hype, it stays buried. So, the key we need to unlock our heart so to find the treasure within is first of all simplicity...

Pilgrim) Could you please continue?

Father) A traditional monk today should be your role model. So, the three monastic virtues are chastity, obedience to an elder, and poverty. This poverty is that simple living where we shed the "extras".

Pilgrim) I didn't know that. What about chastity and obedience? Can that apply to us?

Father) When you obey your father-confessor and do what I am about to tell you on prayer, then you arrive at the doorstep of chaste thinking. Your thoughts will be simple. They will not be fueled by your passions.

Pilgrim) We cannot wait to learn. Please father.

Father) The "according to nature" mode is to live like Jesus. You don't need gadgets in your pocket that produce and promote the highest forms of immorality. The world has been desensitized - it is unrecognizable anymore. Even monks are walking around with these things in their hands instead of the prayer rope. And without any sign of shame. So, when you are rid of these and other "extras" which you don't need, then you can raise yourself - by the grace of God - to another level.

Pilgrim) But society says otherwise.

Father) Then go ahead and do what society tells you to do. I do not want to conform. Even if I were in the world, I would find ways to live simply. And there are ways. Plant a garden also, go for a walk, eat right, and say the prayer, "Lord Jesus Christ have mercy on me." This Jesus Prayer along with the poverty of the spirit will make you light on your feet, and you will be able someday to fly over this cuckoo's nest that is built around us.

Pilgrim) But I like where I am and what I am doing. Though sometimes I do get the blues.

Father) It is nice that you love the world in which you live. But simplify and be thankful. After these, the next step is to learn to repeat the Jesus Prayer orally, at all times. This should take care of the blues considering that you also confess, honor your parents, and all people.

Pilgrim) We all do these things. And we call on Jesus.

Father) During noetic prayer then, it is good to have found a quiet place to be sitting, and to create a gentle atmosphere...

Pilgrim) If I may say, now that I remember, I do find tears sometimes when I thank the Lord.

Father) Good. A thankful feeling for all of God's blessings will warm the heart so it will be receptive to His love. And after you find a good spot in your home and have created this atmosphere, you will sit and repeat the Jesus Prayer with the lips, quietly and with a sense of love for God. Do not overly worry the technology, it has a place in your lives. Do what you can is what I am saying. But usually, people who are avid phone users will not be able to pray for a long time. If you want to help yourself cut the time you are on it for the reason that impressions you may gather will lead to distractions during prayer.

Pilgrim) I have read, as you say, that monks don't follow trends.

Father) It goes without saying. Monks go to a monastery to find something that the Holy Fathers speak about. They go to find sanctity. Can you imagine St. Anthony being hooked up with that sort of thing? In his pocket? We have to pray, boys. The world is coming to an end, I suppose.

Pilgrim) What can we do for these distractions that float around during the time of prayer?

Father) The evil one will always fight us with images. Man thinks as he imagines and so the fantasy is the devil's best weapon that he uses against us. But again, if we cut down the intake of impressions and we take direction from our teacher, then the images will be fewer, that's for sure.

Pilgrim) Did you say that prayer of the heart can become unceasing?

Father) Again, we have so much to thank God for. Think of it as if some billionaire gave you a few million as a gift. What would you do? Think about him day and night with tears in your eyes. But here, we have a soul that is worth more than the universe! How grateful must we be? So, approach Jesus in your little prayer spot with gratitude as you repeat the Jesus Prayer. That will set the tone for your rule and for the rest of your day.

Pilgrim) What do you mean by rule?

Father) Since you asked me about the "prayer of the heart," I am giving you a rule, some guidelines to go by so you will find some grace and peace.

Pilgrim) You have called this prayer, could you comment?

Father) This is called noetic prayer, or circular prayer, by the neptic saints. It is also called pure because it is done without the imagination - pure of thoughts, concepts, ideas, whims, memories - in the heart. When the heart gets warmed up and one starts shedding tears, the nous unites and fantasy subsides. This naturally happens to all, but it does not last for long. Well, there is a method and techniques which help to prolong this fantasy-free, warm-hearted and blessed feeling.

Pilgrim) You have promised, Father, now tell us about this method.

Father) Sure. But first, I insist that you live normal lives, breaking a sweat, camping, jogging, boating, appreciating, as I have discussed, every little thing, and simplifying your ways. And finding the time to pray, that too.

Pilgrim) We promise. After all, we are not strangers to prayer, but we do want to learn more.

Father) Have you read St. Gregory Palamas or St. Nikodemos of the Holy Mountain? Do you understand the saying: "Descend with your nous to the heart?" I want to know where you are in all this.

Pilgrim) If I may answer you, we are readers and we try, but this notion of the nous descending...

Father) Once you learn what the nous is it will be like: "Look mom! No hands!" Listen carefully, it is not so hard to understand. The nous is the focus, the attention, the awareness. When we feel a certain part of our body, there goes the nous. When we have a toothache the nous/attention is there on the tooth. So, when the Fathers say, "put your nous at the heart" they are really saying: "put your attention there, your awareness, or focus." And when we put all of our attention/focus on the place where our physical heart is situated, somewhere close by there, then the imagination stops.

Pilgrim) And our prayer becomes pure. Is that all?

Father) Believe it or not. This is not some strange practice that some of today's "experts" claim it to be. Don't you see the fans and the players during the singing of the national anthem? With their hand at their heart? The heart is the organ of emotion and love. When you love someone, the heart utters ineffable cries toward that one you have in mind. Sometimes when you pray while feeling your heart, the eyes well-up and fantasy is eliminated.

Pilgrim) What are some ways to help feel our hearts?

Father) OK. The nous is the attention, that feeling which helps to locate a body part without the use of the hands, right? So then when we breathe into our lung area, along with the air, we bring our nous/attention down there and it adheres there by sensation.

Pilgrim) I am starting to understand as I do this.

Father) If you breathe in, where the breath stops, this is where the heart is. Breathe in and stop for a few seconds to get an idea of what it feels like down there...

Pilgrim) Very interesting. And very easy.

Father) After placing the nous at, or somewhere around the heart, the next step is to find the inner logos. You know that little voice we put to use to read books, to write essays, and to think silently. This is the voice of the heart. We give to this voice God's Holy Name to pronounce - inside of us - along with the sense of gratitude that we spoke of earlier.

Pilgrim) Do we have to breathe in to locate the spot we want our nous to be?

Father) Initially yes. As time goes on and you do this exercise you might want to combine the Jesus Prayer to every inhalation and then by saying it as you exhale. Thus, the breath and the holy words unite and travel to and fro and then back in and out of your lungs. So, you can try this on for size. The advantage of saying the Jesus Prayer, by breathing it in and out of you, is that the Jesus Prayer can become automatic when joined to the breath because the breath is automatic and goes on its own. These two, the breath and prayer, make a great pair.

Pilgrim) I have read about this technique in the "Counsels from the Holy Mountain".

Father) An excellent book to read... well, I hear the bells for vespers, God bless you, I hope we'll meet again... By the way, where do you come from? What do you do?

Pilgrim) We are from the U.S.; we teach at an Ivy league school... at Yale.

Father) Awesome. I myself went to Harvard. There I learned to pray.

Pilgrim) ??

ACROSS THE BORDER

Mr. Rodriguez) I have spent years in the U.S. where I studied and worked in universities. Before that I was in Europe, in Spain, and I lived in a monastery for approximately eighteen years. There I became acquainted with the inner life of an Orthodox monk. I almost became one, to tell you the truth.

Tourist) How did you end up in Spain?

Mr. Rodriguez) My brother was the abbot of a skete on the outskirts of Barcelona - a northeastern seaport - and I was then alone, at the tender age of nine. So, he sent for me.

Tourist) What happened to your parents, if I may ask?

Mr. Rodriguez) They died in a plague. My uncle raised me and put me to work in his Cantina. I don't remember playing with the other children. All I did was work; cleaning, busing tables, washing pots and pans, doing dishes, mopping floors, that sort of thing. And I studied - I loved to read. In school I excelled.

Tourist) Did you like monastery life. How was the environment there? Did you learn to pray?

Mr. Rodriguez) At first I was introduced to a daily strict rule of prayer, reading scripture, making prostrations, attending church. And I had a good teacher, Father John, who taught me how to behave there along with the other thirteen monks. He also taught me several Latin-based languages and the Bible, starting with the primordial fall. It was very interesting.

Tourist) Do you want to tell me about it?

Mr. Rodriguez) The fall of Adam and Eve, and death, came by way of disobedience. Therefore, a monk strives to bring back this state of blessedness, which was lost by the transgression, through obedience. Through obedience man restores his relationship with God the Father. And a monk becomes like Adam again. The lustful/carnal passions which maliciously assault humankind cannot find a place to be in an Orthodox monastery because of the obedience of a monastic to the abbot. Adam and Eve were celibate and pure as only the monks, or nuns, are able to remain chaste today, almost eight thousand years after the fall, precisely because of their submission to the Church and to an elder.

Tourist) So purity is a fruit of obedience?

Mr. Rodriguez) Yes. And also, prayer is a fruit.

Tourist) Could you tell me about this? Prayer is a topic on the top of my list for discussion. I am very interested.

Mr. Rodriguez) Prayer is innate in us. A human needs to talk to his Maker; he needs to communicate with God. But please let me take it from the beginning: Christ was Adam's prototype. Adam was created in His image physically and spiritually. We see in the icons, which depict man's creation, an Adam who looks exactly like Christ as he receives His breath by which his soul is fashioned, having rational faculties, and attributes, and aspects resembling those of the One True God Who Is. Then Eve was created in the image of Adam, who again, is the image of Christ Who Himself is the image of God. Therefore, there is a strong connection between a Great God and this little man who walks the earth.

Tourist) I was very eager to hear about prayer. But so far, as you are going round about, I am feeling that this is the best way to approach this subject.

Mr. Rodriguez) What I am trying to say is that, to quote St. Nicetas Stethatos, "A soul desires and seeks to be united with God from Whom it had its origin." But it cannot do this since the mind is defiled. So, to pray effectively we must cleanse the mind first and our heart so to be conditioned to receive the grace of prayer. The Saints agree that this purity is achieved by repentance. With heartfelt repentance a man's communication with God resumes and even gets stronger with time…

Tourist) Go on please, I am listening.

Mr. Rodriguez) The inner need we all have as humans to pray comes from a grace with which our soul is endowed at conception. This special grace, or what is defined in the Greek language as a gift, manifests itself by a live conscience and exhibits of the fear of God and the longing to know God. This trio proves to me that we are not self-propelled or independent in the broader sense of the word but are governed by

200

principles and rules of conduct which help our mind to be in a proper state and to not digress from its own dignity and nature.

Tourist). I have heard it said once that our salvation is a free gift.

Mr. Rodriguez) And so is prayer. Everything is a gift. And even after we sin, God gave us repentance to make it right again, to appease our conscience. Saint Diadochos Photikis writes that in our conscience dwells God. And so, He pulls "the strings" by His fear and the longing to know and be with Him. If we obey, everything goes smoothly so we are also happy, and we pray well.

Tourist) Ahh... happiness, those were the days. When I was a child praying with mom in front of the icons, I was so, so full of joy. But tell me how do monks pray? And what was their regimen there in Spain, in the monastery?

Mr. Rodriguez) The schedule of services in the monastery of the Theotokos included morning and evening services, a meal twice a day, and manual work as much as each monk could handle. Don't forget that this was a time before the introduction of technology, and monastery life was the real deal. Today if you take the phone away from a monk, he is liable to leave his place of repentance. We live in the end times.

Tourist) Was it peaceful there, with a prayerful atmosphere?

Mr. Rodriguez). Very. It was like a paradise would be described except for the few buildings scattered between the gardens, within the forest area, with an open gazebo, the Church, and a barn housing a handful of goats, a donkey, a pair of cats and a shepherd dog named Toby. At this blessed place lived Greek monks, Spaniards, a Frenchman and an old Russian father who had escaped imprisonment and the firing squad.

He taught me to pray with the Jesus Prayer but in Russian. I also learned to speak Russian...

Tourist) You mean he taught you to pray with "Lord Jesus Christ have mercy on me?" This is called mental prayer.

Mr. Rodriguez) That's right. Except that he did not say the whole prayer but only the name Jesus. He would repeat it under his breath, sometimes quietly. He had what is called prayer in the heart, confiding to my lowliness that he heard the Lord's Name inside him at all times, it went on its own. He told me to say the whole Prayer. And so much joy did it give me that it seems that I walked another world. Nothing bothered me - I was then around twelve.

Tourist) I have read about prayer in the heart and how it goes of its own accord. Yet I don't know what to make of it. How does it repeat in one's head? Can you elucidate the matter?

Mr. Rodriguez) Man's heart and mind is created in Christ's image. As I understand it, the Jesus Prayer is built into our system, as is God's law. What did He say? God is within us. The Lord Himself said this before the arrival of Pentecost. Then St. John in his gospel, chapter two, says that the Word/Jesus enlightens every man that comes into the world. He said, "every man," did you notice? So, by our baptism the Lord went into our hearts and unlocked this treasure - His Name - which we had inherited at birth. So, when you find a quiet spot try this: start by saying the Jesus Prayer rhythmically, "Lord... Jesus Christ... have mercy on me..." Do this a few times and then let go, and the prayer will likely continue on its own.

Tourist) Could it be that easy?

Mr. Rodriguez) Do not be amazed if it starts going on its own right now as we speak or while you are sleeping, without any effort on your part. The Jesus Prayer has been resounding in my head since we met at the park. But of course, it has been going on for years now by the grace of God and the blessing of my starets.

Tourist) And this is an on-going occurrence?

Mr. Rodriguez) Nonstop. But I am careful. I have been fortunate to grow up in a monastery and I know about the watchfulness needed for a man to stay chaste. I am also a subdeacon, and I am always in Church.

Tourist). I am married. My wife and children are waiting for me at the Hotel. When will I find that quiet time needed to pray thus? Also, there is the purity that you have mentioned. Isn't this a factor, considering that I do not have the purity of a monk?

Mr. Rodriguez) In marriage the thoughts should have a better character - this is possible. And you can find the time if you really want to learn to pray. God does not play favorites; He loves everyone the same. I say find that quiet five minutes, yes five minutes only at first until you acquire the taste for prayer. You will be very surprised to see yourself be drawn to this special time and slowly but surely you will come to love it.

Tourist) You know Mr. Rodriguez; I should do this. I want to thank you for your wisdom, you give me hope. I have neglected my soul for years now... well, here is our hotel.

Mr. Rodriguez) It has been a real pleasure, David. God bless.

Youth) The other day, Father, I was playing with my sister's son, who is four years old, and I was shocked to hear something very inappropriate coming out of his mouth. His dad also heard this.

PriestMonk) I can imagine what must have been his reaction.

Youth) This child does not watch T.V. or play with electronics. I came to ask you specifically about this. I am perplexed.

Monk) Don't be. The words which a man hears go into memory and they are then spoken orally without his consent. Most times they are inaudible. One hears cursing, blaspheming of the worst kind and he thinks to himself, "Am I losing it?" A child is no different except that because of his immaturity, it slips out of his lips for everyone to hear. And he does not really know what he is saying either.

Youth) Should we not be alarmed?

Monk) What his parents should do is to give their offspring good things to hear. What a human sees and hears goes to his nous and it can pollute or sanctify it. Unfortunately, people today are not in touch with reality and have other diversions to deal with.

Youth) Such as?

Monk) Making money, recreation, sports for the young. The list is a mile long. But spiritually they are famished. Even in Church, where the grace of God abounds, we have low levels of conscious apprehension of essential truths. What I mean is that our faith lacks a practical application. We read aplenty but...

Youth) Please enlighten me, Father. I want to know more about my faith. Teach me.

Monk) God will teach you all things in time. As for me, what I can do is help you to find Him. So, you start by being good to your parents; this is a must. And you have to find some time to devote to prayer. You have to confess regularly and take Holy Communion worthily. Otherwise, wait until you are somewhat blameless.

Youth) Isn't Holy Communion the antidote to death; will it not heal me where I stumble and give me spiritual health?

Monk) The Lord's Body and Blood is fire for the unworthy. You have to prepare yourself. Spend a few minutes by reading a few lines of the Akathist and do not approach the Holy Chalice nonchalantly. I would say with confidence that if you do only these few basic things the road will open wide, and you will travel with ease. Now, there are things you can do to stay focused so as to not lose zeal, because the devil is going to fight you.

Youth) I'm listening.

Monk) The nous - the mind that is - which is found in your heart MUST see holy icons, smell incense, hear church music, taste and touch the Holy Sacraments. It is able to see, smell, hear, taste and touch by way of the senses. The nous itself is safely enclosed in its abode. The eyes, nose, ears, tongue and feeling are instruments the senses associated with them use, so that the mind comes in contact with the outside world.

Youth) So the senses supply the nous with information.

Monk) Correct. And to stay focused and God-loving it must be connected to the right source. If the source is evil, the results are devastating. All this derangement, mania that we see all around us is manifested through folks who are attuned to the wrong frequency, as St. Paisios of the Holy Mountain would say. The nous/mind cannot protect itself without God's help. We need to attract His grace by keeping the Commandments.

Youth) What did you mean, Father, when you said that people are not in touch with reality?

Monk) I mean with the world of the spirits. They do not apprehend this reality because it is unseen to the naked eye, yet we live in it. The little devils make their rounds and they find ways of influence and various mood swings; the heart begins to flutter and change drastically from one moment to the next and the thoughts are coming in. A man starts not feeling good and then falls to the passions to find some relief. This is how it goes.

Youth) The passions cannot soothe a soul. I know this from experience.

Monk) There is pleasure there initially but it turns sour.

Youth) Why is that?

Monk) The conscience gets riled up and then there is no rest. God is saying, "don't do that." If the cravings of the flesh are satisfied to the max, then starts depression, anxiety and all other sorts of disorder. Also, if there are thoughts which come into the nous to linger and find a home, conscience pangs appear out of the blue...

Youth) Excuse me for interrupting. Could you tell me, what is a conscience?

Monk) It is God's voice telling you what to do. And you have to comply, or else. It will not leave you at peace. Now, in the case of your nephew, he is innocent, and he is not old enough to be reproved by his conscience. He does not know what he is doing. As for you and me it's a different story.

Youth) Oh... could you explain?

Monk) Our vocabulary is extensive, you see? And our thought process is more cultivated. When a thought comes up to our brain, out of our heart, we stop to gather ourselves and think about whom we are speaking to, how we might gain the attention of others, and the style to use for a specific purpose. We decide when to speak, how clearly, and for our expression to be approved by our listeners, the words we use must be arranged in the proper sequence.

Youth) We are able to control the quality of our output.

Monk) Exactly. But, you know, even at an advanced old age a slip of the tongue occurs, and quite frequently. After a stressful day at the office, during a bout with depression, a fit of anger, or a moment of frustration. During adversity, temptations, a flat tire... Anyone is liable to fall, at any age. And fall he will. There is no escape.

Youth) What about hope, or a remedy. Something to do. Please Father, think of something, I'm at a loss. I, too, have this problem sometimes.

Monk) Take hold of yourself, my boy. It is all you can do. And do not confront others when you are upset. Do not forget that a human being is surrounded by a spiritual energy field where demons dwell. And this is what happens: during a fit, the mouth, not guarded by the reason, opens and this creates a draft of evil thoughts to go into the heart, to ascend and be spat out of the mouth at an incredible speed, to wound the recipient or whoever is there present at the time.

Youth) It is really sad, to attack someone you love. And this happens often also with other people that I know.

Monk) Sure. And you know what? This is sinful and once you, or whoever, starts to do this they will not stop. They can't. It has become a bad habit. Not unlike a grown child is the person who does not care about others' feelings. But then, such an attitude could serve as a security blanket – don't be surprised. Stepping on others fortifies the ego; makes a man feel strong; it aids in acquiring self-confidence.

Youth) Wow! At what depths of abasement a body falls.

Monk) Now you know yourself, as the ancients used to say. Go on and sin no more. Guard your eyes and ears and those of your children, when you become a father, from the impropriety of this age; secure your mouth and mind.

Youth) Thank you, Father. I am going to try. Your blessing… Goodbye.

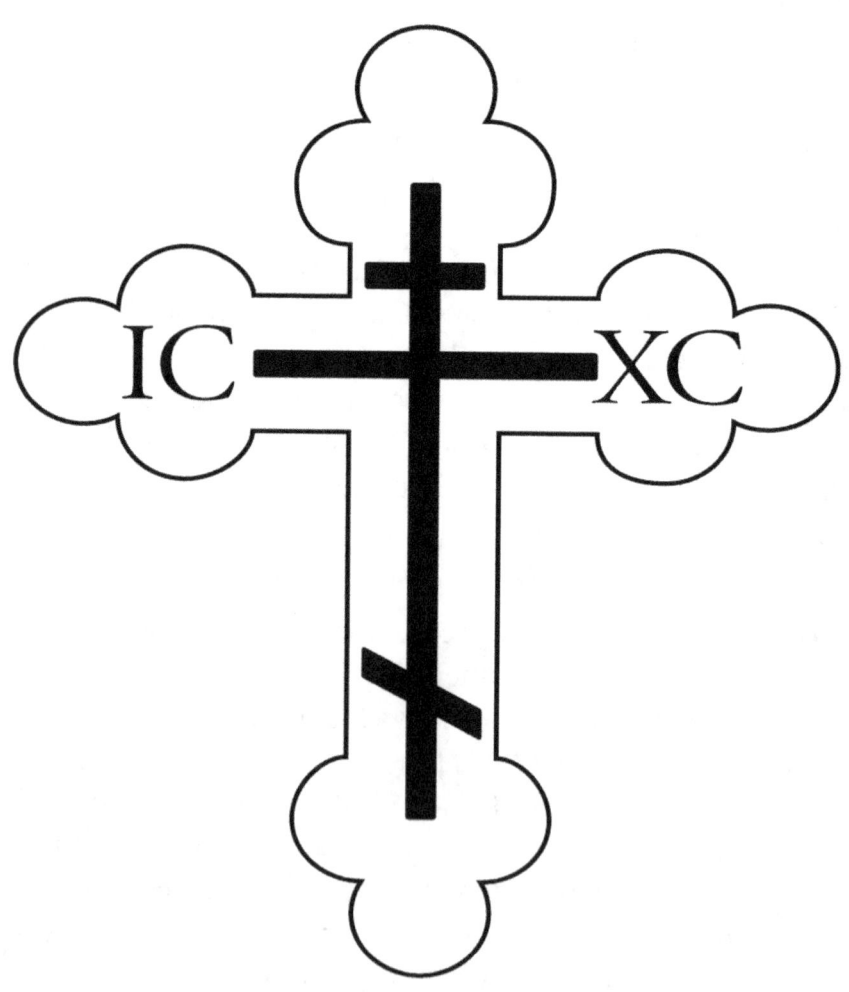

... and thither, nor their thoughts in fact, but the awareness (to use this word for now) is something that someone can move at will, to tranfer the nous at any time and to do so by sensation! Sense perception is governed by the nous at the heart who is "boss", the "Inner man", the "eye of the soul", the Image of God in us. When we feel a certain part in our body the nous/focus goes there immediately and because we are now attentive/aware of that spot, the brain at the head malfunctions. Thus the evil one cannot present to us his filthy scenarios, schemes and the rest of the trash. Pure prayer starts from here: to feel the place where our physical heart is situated and to adhere there by our attention to alleviate distraction which appears during prayer, and at other times. The monk always feels his heart and can sense by its movement the type of the temptation that he will be assaulted shortly thereafter. He cannot take chances.

Q) Father, I don't understand. Please do something. Could you explain it to me?

A) Prayer is like any other trade. To learn you must go to school and live in a monastery a few years, with temptations, with thoughts, with self-denial and nightly vigils, or read some books and make believe that you know something. Most people do this today after being received in the Church with only Chrismation: the very next day they are writing their own book. So, to learn and to understand you must be trained by a licensed professional, you know, a monk. Otherwise stay at your level, read some devotionals from a prayer book and love your neighbor. Do not kid yourself thinking that you are something which, obviously, you are not.

Q) I have read the Holy Fathers and I do understand quite a bit but what eludes me is the material associated with the prayer of the intellect.

A) There is no such thing as prayer of the intellect. If you meant to say prayer of the nous or heart, that is different. The intellect cannot pray. It is the power of man's reason which helps to process all sorts of information that comes up out of the heart to the brain, and makes conclusions which are used, or go into memory, depending on the occasion at hand. Intellectual productions are not always manifested orally but sometimes they are kept hidden. This can result in mental and/or physical illness.

Q) Could you explain?

A) The intellect makes rational conclusions. And the evil one fights us this way. A man's reason is swayed by passion. Pride does not let us reveal bad thoughts to our priest because we figure that he will reprove us or see us differently. And because evil thoughts are propelled by demonic energy, this energy stays with us, and with time the thoughts become wounds.

Q) So, what can we do to reason in a better way, a God-fearing way?

A) Go and be a monastic to cut your will. Let your intellect conform to the intellect of another man and the products of your brain will not fight you. Your thoughts will be his thoughts. Under obedience you will come to say to yourself, "If that is what the elder wants, this is what I want." When the power of reason gets used to not making its own decisions then the soul is liberated from the tyranny of the passions.

Q) But I am married. What now?

A) Obey your spouse to some extent, obey your priest, obey the Church, obey your boss, obey the laws. But you have to obey with your heart, not typically. Like as if you want to obey. Make an effort to also obey the weather.

Q) The weather!!!?

A) Yes. When it snows, make believe that this is what you want the weather to be that day. If it rains say to yourself, "I love this rain." If it's sunny, "this is what I want." If it is foggy, so be it. Don't go against God's plan for that particular day. If you give in and you accept and surrender your will to undesired climate conditions, then you will be at peace. Otherwise, don't expect God to give you grace. Your desire must adjust with what He offers, and you must approve.

Q) This way of thinking is new to us. But please continue.

A) Ever since the fall of Adam, our will does not align with the will of our Heavenly Father, and that is why we are not happy. You asked me about prayer, but I must first try to explain that man's reason now cannot come to terms with the existing reality that troubles, pain, tribulation and grief is our lot on

211

earth until we die. The intellect is baffled as to why such a loving God lets us suffer this way.

Q) I have thought about this many a time. I think you have the answer. Can you tell us about it?

A) This whole scenario of living in adversity and sorrow does not make sense because man thinks wrong and does wrong, our Christians included. According to St. Paul there is the spiritual man and the carnal man. The carnal man is flesh and the flesh lusts against the spirit and the spirit goes against the flesh. So, the intellect and the whole mechanism of thinking and cogitation has been corrupted, and it has become "flesh". So, the thoughts of modern man revolve around the self-gratification of the body and the senses. He even prays to feel good physically, to be stimulated because that is what he knows. Especially in this hedonistic society we live in the Americas. To turn this way of thinking around...

Q) We are all ears, Father...

A) One must crucify the flesh with its passions and desires. And he or she will do this by giving in to Divine authority and design. Everyone knows what to do. The Law is written in a human heart. So let us all take it one day at a time to turn into a spiritual person by accepting what God gave us. Are we tall, short, chubby, bald? Accept who we are - we cannot fight God. And be grateful for everything; for our families, our siblings, our friends, for the food we eat, for our home, for our country, for our Orthodoxy. And of course, for the weather.

Q) We will then taste the fruits of the Spirit. Isn't that right? The gospel says so.

A) A spiritual person tastes spiritual fruits. Like love, joy, peace, long-suffering, kindness, goodness, faithfulness, gentleness, self-control. Notice the same Holy Apostle says "longsuffering" in the same chapter, five I believe, there in Galatians? Longsuffering includes patience, and meekness, which is a necessary virtue to acquire happiness. What did our Lord say? "Know from me that I am meek and lowly of heart and you will find rest in your souls."

Q) Is there a connection between the rest of soul and prayer?

A) You must have clairvoyance (smiles) because this is the point that I had in mind to bring up. A man of God who finds this rest prays all day, and all night, if you can believe this. When Saints come upon this grace, not only they do not cower against everyday adversity and hardship, but they want to suffer more! They are now on another level. Monastics are numb to pain, even those simple novices who dig and clean the latrine, because they have this grace.

Q) Tell us again how this comes about?

A) Through obedience, thankfulness, contentment, and confession with sincere repentance is also a must. But you must also put your two mites into some form of prayer so that the aforementioned becomes a reality you live with. And then slowly but surely it goes under your skin, and instead of nagging and moaning about your shortcomings and/or difficulties you now start appreciating and stop rationalizing. The snake of old is hiding within your power of reason. Stop thinking and start thanking is what I'm trying to say.

Q) What kind of prayers do you suggest that we read?

A) All prayers are good: morning and evening prayers, akathists, paraklesis, the Lord's Prayer and also prayers using your own words to talk to Him Whom you love, your Maker who brought us all to being from nothing. And then there is the Theotokos prayer: "Most Holy Theotokos save us" and the Jesus Prayer: "Lord Jesus Christ have mercy on me." This prayer is the best because it contains the Name of Jesus before

Whom every knee shall bow, in the Heavens, in hell and on earth.

Q) So, is this the prayer of the nous?

A) Now you're talking. The intellect we talked about cannot be nous. The nous is something else: it is found in the core of one's existence within the physical heart, and it is the image of God in man who is created free and rational. All animate and inanimate species have life within them, but they don't have a rational nous. Only humans have this which is called the "eye of the soul" because it apprehends both the physical and spiritual realities with senses that are akin to each. The nous can see, feel, desire, decide, and act incorporeally but also physically as it has the senses at its disposal and by extension, the brain, the muscles and limbs. When the nous is healthy it is the absolute sovereign, judge and jury; the CEO at company headquarters; the Boss. But now it is ailing. And the prayer of the nous or what is called otherwise noetic prayer helps to heal it.

Q) It is very sad that it is ill. Please tell us why it is so.

A) The nous is a spirit. No one but God knows what it is made of. It is the purest part of the soul and the mind of the soul, if you will. Thus, the soul is alive, free, and rational because it has a faculty that thinks. The thoughts come to the nous from four sources: the senses, the memory, the body's temperament, and the devil who is the cause of all evil. He does not have authority over us but what he does is to sow evil desires into our nous as we grow up so that later he can influence the soul into committing sins allied to those desires. His intention is to finally take us down to Hell for all eternity.

Q) Oh boy!... But now, how is it healed, Father?

A) Since the soul is in disarray and the Desire/Volition aspect of the nous wants things that God does not want, the aspect of

214

the nous which is the Intelligence/Cognition, recognizes the danger of sinning and confronts the Desire with arguments against this provocation. If the Intelligence cannot effectively do this, the Incensive/Willpower aspect of the nous must come in and use force to stabilize the situation and stop the sin from occurring, to bring peace back into the soul. These three aspects, or powers, must be in agreement for the soul to be healthy. For this, obedience is needed as we have discussed earlier, and the Jesus Prayer. Now, we cannot clean the heart in one day, but we struggle and try to get better slowly.

Q) Did you not mention some other things along with obedience?

A) Yes. Under the virtue of obedience fall the other virtues; those of patience, repentance, meekness, longsuffering, love. Our Lord, with obedience, opened the Paradise we had lost by disobedience. The key is obedience, the humble are obedient and they perform miracles by God's grace because God obeys those who obey, and He listens to them. The monks deliberately cut their will to attract the grace of God. A man, by obedience, can head back to the state of Adam and acquire dispassion. Remember? What did we say about the intellect and reason? Obedience smashes this evil that thinks we can do it ourselves, our self-reliance, which is a product of reason.

Q) Self-reliance?

A) This is the idea the snake planted in the head of the protoplasts, the first people: that they can be gods without God. That they do not need to obey a higher order. But now we Christians, we know that this can't be. We are driven either by God's benevolent care or by the destructive forces of darkness. We choose. But since we live in a fallen state, we choose wrong most of the time. So, we give rights to the evil one to approach us and the two natural instincts we have of reproduction and self-preservation are perverted.

Q) And we see this in the world today, how man is manipulated by the dark one.

A) Of course. In order to preserve ourselves as our Lord would want, He gave us a bit of love for ourselves. But this love grew and became egoism fueled by pride and arrogance. The Holy Fathers say that self-love is the mother of all the passions. An excess of self-love, that is: we all have to defend and protect ourselves and we should have some kind of respect and love for our being, but too much is not good.

Q) If we don't like our person, why would we strive to be saved?

A) Correct. Even I, as a monk, when I reach out to help someone, I make sure that I am not in jeopardy. The soul is not something a man can gamble with; it is a great gift from God, and we must protect it like we would protect our baby. Actually, when we sin, we deprive our soul of that loving care it needs to stay alive in God, and healthy. The Jesus Prayer keeps the demons at bay to a great extent and helps to plant in our mind the right amount of love, along with the idea that we cannot do it ourselves. "Lord Jesus Christ have mercy on me." We say "have mercy on me" because without God we cannot live, we cannot love, we cannot do anything!

Q) You are right, we cannot rely on our "muscle." Could you tell us now how to use the Jesus Prayer to help us stay sinless?

A) This holy prayer is closely connected to watchfulness. Watchfulness or vigilance is to look out always for trouble before it begins. The nous has the ability, if it is trained properly, to shuffle away any unwanted thoughts straightaway at their conception. But let us first take a look at the other dimension, the world of the spirits. The demons press against our heart trying to come in with this or that pretense. They want to come into us and then rise to the head so to take over our reason. And because our power of reason is ill and leans most times toward the sinful life, as I have already explained, we are in danger 24/7.

Q) Does the Name of God watch out for us?

A) Yes. It watches, guards and prevents. When we say the Prayer, the dark spirits are going crazy. They cannot stand to hear this Name. Especially when it is repeated inwardly inside oneself. Interior prayer has great value because it confronts the devil at the source where he appears and destroys his schemes. Everyone should say the Jesus Prayer, every man, woman, and child. Every Christian, Orthodox Christian, everyone who is baptized or chrismated, all catechumens, and even those who inquire about the faith: everyone. St. John in chapter two of his holy gospel says that the Word enlightens every man who comes into the world. Every man. Please, do not prevent the name Jesus from being heard. Those of you who serve at the Church, say the Prayer inside of you or under your breath. You have no right to tell others not to utter the sweet Name of the Lord or that it's not for them, or some other kind of nonsense. This is what the demons want, for prayer to stop so that they can do their work.

Q) We didn't know that the Jesus Prayer should be said at all times and in all places.

A) Well, now you know. If you were a monk and you reasoned yourself out of saying the Jesus Prayer, the demons would play volleyball with your head. When we speak about spiritual matters let us be sure of what comes out of our lips. Let us be prudent. For the Catechumens - in this special case - they should learn to stand or sit before the Lord One-on-one to say the Prayer every day along with the morning and evening prayers.

Q) We would like to thank you so much for your wisdom.

On Repentance

The mystery of repentance does wonderful things when we reveal our passions, weaknesses, shortcomings and complexes clearly and sincerely to a priest. The grace of God, which is present and overtly active in this most salvific sacrament, cannot be felt or evaluated by reason, but rather by faith alone. After repentance we must not look back but put everything behind us and with the help of a modest lifestyle and the broom of prayer, as it were, we will sweep bad memories aside. Then, to get rid of the stains of past mistakes, sins and trauma we can use the elbow grease of patience and forbearance toward everyone, and the cleansing action of tears.

SPIRITUAL AWARENESS TEST II

We can find Scriptural topics for discussion as we drink our tea on a quiet evening, or when we entertain guests.

Difference between rosary prayer and prayer rope prayer.
Fantasy and muddled thought versus undistractedness and clarity of thought.

Does a monk-recluse have much freedom?
Not really. His movement is limited within a boundary he has freely set for himself.

Who was the first Bishop of Jerusalem?
St. James, the Lord's brother.

Name the famous Theological school in France.
St. Sergius Seminary.

Why does a Saint strive for self-control?
Self-control is pleasing to God because a person can stay blameless.

Where did Saint Nectarios become a monk?
On the Greek island of Chios.

What country's Patriarch is called "Catholicos"?
The country of Georgia.

Do folks get married during Great Lent?
No.

What are the Orthodox who are non-canonical?
These are schismatics.

Give two reasons why imagination is bad.
Imagination is the bridge of the demons.
One cannot control the mind with imagination.

Who compiled the Philokalia?
Saint Nicodemos of the Holy Mountain.

What did St. Diadochos say about the conscience?
God dwells in man's conscience.

Which of the two hands is rarely used in Holy Altar?
The left hand.

Why did God allow the Turks to take Constantinople?
There was the danger of union with the Papacy. Under the Turks, we remained Orthodox.

How many monasteries established in U.S. since 1980?
About eighty.

If this is what Geronda wants, it's what I want?
This is how an obedient monk thinks.

Is unceasing prayer something to strive for?
Yes. It is a need we cannot do without.

Jesus Christ Who was God, appeared as a servant?
(Philippians 2:6-8) Our Lord came in the likeness of a man and humbled himself.

What is the most popular pilgrimage in Greece?
The Panagia Evangelistria Church in Tinos.

What is the most sacred place in the world?
Our Lord's Holy Sepulchre in the Church of the Resurrection in Jerusalem.

Where was the plant basil found? (meaning of the King)
At the base of the True Precious Cross when it was discovered, whence it got its name.

Are there any Chinese Saints in China?
There are quite a few.

In how many languages has the Bible been translated?
In over twenty-eight hundred languages (2,883 to be exact).

Name a very famous Bulgarian hermit-Saint.
Saint John of Rila.

What do fathers call the "art of arts and science of sciences?"
The famous Noetic prayer.

Did Jesus Christ speak Greek to the people?
Most likely. There were Greek cities (Decapolis) and many Greek-speaking Jews.

How did Jericho fall to the Israelites?
Jericho's walls crumbled. The city was seized easily.

Whose incorrupt relics are found in San Francisco?
Saint John Maximovich of Shanghai and San Francisco.

How long did it take to build Solomon's temple?
Seven years.

What is meaning of the Greek word "Ekklesia" (Church)?
It means the "gathering" or "assembly."

Who is Saint Nikolai Velimirovich?

A superb Serbian spiritual writer, poet, and a Bishop-Confessor during World War II.

Who was the only non-priest to enter the Holy place?
The Theotokos lived in the Holy place of Solomon's temple (Holy of Holies) for twelve years.

Why does Orthodoxy flourish in third world countries?
Hard living conditions help establish faith in the hearts of the people.

Was Saint Rupert Scandinavian?
No. He was actually a German pre-schism saint.

Why were the Hebrews such fierce fighters?
They were feared by everyone because they had God with them.

How long did it take the wise men to go to Bethlehem?
Over two years after the appearance of the rising star.

Give a good reason why monastics find prayer.
Self-denial.

What are the "vain repetitions" Bible is referring to?

The correct translation is "incoherent babbling" as the idolaters became possessed in worship.

Show the way to read prayer book undistractedly.

Put your index finger under the line you are reading and move it along as you read the words.

How do we prove that we have faith?

By our good works.

Name two Romanian Confessors who died in the US.

Frs. Roman Braga and George Calciu.

The word "husband" is not found in Scripture.

"Andra" (literally "man") can either denote marriage, or betrothal as in the case of Joseph.

What are the three main temptations or vices?

Love of pleasure, avarice, vainglory.

What's the sneakier of the seven deadly sins?

Acedia. It is negligence, listlessness, dejection, depression - a mixed bag.

What was the real name of Joshua, son of Nun?

Jesus. This is the name ascribed to
him in the Old Testament, the same
as our Lord.

Who was Moses' oldest sister?
Miriam, an important leader during
the Exodus.

Do monastics eat meat or chicken?
No, they do not.

**List two good things gained from being
stubborn.**
A strong will power and hope for a
future with Christ in Paradise.

What do all the Saints have in common?
A great love for the Mother of God.

**An unthought-of but sure way to attract
God's love.**
Show your appreciation for every
little thing in life.

Who destroyed Jerusalem and when?
Titus, before himself becoming
Emperor, destroyed it in 70 AD (under
his father, Emperor Vespasian).

**What did St. Paul point out in chapter 7 of
Romans?**
That, at times, we are incapable of
doing what we want to do. We are
ill.

Can you explain what it means to descend by nous to the heart?

It is to have the focus and all your attention on the physical organ of the heart.

Who was named the "father of Orthodoxy"?
St. Athanasios the Great.

"Proskinesis" in Scripture does not always mean "worship."

It translates as "bowing, veneration, worship." It depends on the intentions of the one bowing.

Hebrew law of retribution was "eye for an eye." Why?

This was fair. It prevented the punishment from exceeding the measure of wrong committed.

Which of Noah's sons was the ancestor of Abraham?

Shem.

Alexander the Great dismounted for the Hebrew High-priest.

He had great respect for the nation and the faith of Israel. He met the High-Priest in Jerusalem.

Who is considered the Father of Monasticism in the West?

Saint Benedict of Nursia.

Why should we not argue with heretics?

Even if you eventually win the argument, the residue of wrong views will remain in the mind.

Where did Lazarus die a second and final time?

Lazarus, the brother of Martha and Mary, became a bishop in Cyprus and died there.

Was St. John the Baptist a relative of Jesus?

Yes, a second cousin. His father Zachariah brought the three-year-old Panagia into the temple.

Where was Pontius Pilate from?

He was from Pontos (Northern Turkey, by the Black Sea).

Was St. Ephraim the Syrian ordained a bishop?

No, he remained in the rank of deacon.

Other devotionals to the Theotokos beside the Akathist?

The Small and Great Parakleses.

THE RETURN TO THE HEART

(Continued from page 5)

- The monk-hesychast flees from the temptation to examine any thought while praying, knowing that any image which appears during prayer is evil.
- Considering this helps him to stay alert and reject any and all conceptual images that come to mind.
- To descend with "the nous energy" to heart level so to unite it with the "nous essence" is to start being conscious, aware and attentive upon the physical organ of the heart and focused there.
- To feel, that is, the place where the heart is situated. The feeling/sensation is the unity.
- And thus, the nous returns to its Source at the heart (the nous essence) and the imaginative mechanism at the head ceases to operate.
- The "why" of it is the purification of the thought process and the illumination of the soul as Saint Hesychios explains in the Philokalia.
- To learn how to make the connection of nous and heart, one must understand that the "nous energy", or awareness, attention, or focus, as it happens to be, does move about by this feeling/sensation. And he who is praying can direct it at will to any part of the body that he chooses.
- One controls the thoughts consciously and brings about stillness to the cerebral haven by directing the nous (attention, focus) away from the head to stop the fantasy.
- For the imagination/fantasy to produce its images it needs the "nous energy" to nestle mostly up at the head.

228

- Now then, when the hesychast "feels" his heart (nous essence), the nous energy has returned to the heart.
- It is that simple! To put the nous in the heart is to "feel" the heart.
- When there is love for God, contrition and tears that means that the unity of nous and heart has been achieved, and evil thoughts have vanished.
- But to prolong that connection for long periods of time as is the ideal for monastics, the Holy Fathers found other ways and methods.
- So, they recommend for the breath to take up the nous and guide it inside the chest. As the air goes into the lung area by the heart, the focus/attention/awareness keeps the nous there in confinement as if in a prison.
- When one loses the awareness of that spot that the nous is resting in, that means that the nous has escaped to the outside and the unity has been lost as well as the peace, and the undistractedness.
- Then, demonic assaults resume, escorted by many correlating images.
- So once again: the breath guides the nous toward the heart through the breathing canal, where the breath stops, that is where the place of the heart is, and the nous adheres to that place by sensation.
- The nous can tangibly feel a part of the body and by its awareness it can remain there.
- It "touches," calms, and soothes an aching heart hands-free and also prays at the same time inside the cavity of one's chest with the inner voice.
- When the grace of God abounds, the nous sticks at the heart or in the near vicinity of this area, bringing about calmness, tears, and love for God.

- If the attention does not remain inside the chest along with the Jesus Prayer, the nous can attach to the air inhaled and exhaled to keep from wandering.

THE DIALOGUES, PART 4

A DIALOGUE WITH A MONK ABOUT NOETIC PRAYER - FOURTH TALK

Q) Now Father, I remembered you said something about the "return of the nous to itself." Could you explain this further, please?

A) I've mentioned this in the past very briefly. The nous scatters. This is the tragedy of post-fall modern man. As a prodigal son then, it returns to its home to find rest. As an example, we have a steam engine and the steam coming up, as the nous comes up out of the heart, is gathered and led back down. Or the heat produced by a fire rising up to be dispersed into the atmosphere. The fire is the nous in the heart, and the heat is also the nous which springs out of the source, the heart. Well, the nous-heat returns to its source. Keep in mind that the flames of the fire and the heat produced are of the same essence.

Q) And thus, we have essence and energy of the nous?

A) Yes. This essence and energy are of the same substance. The essence of the nous is wholly found inside the heart when a man is unconscious during sleep or in an unconscious state. At this time the brain is idle. As soon as he awakens, the head begins to fill up with the spirit of the nous: the energy. Then, the brain starts conceiving notions, schemes, ideas, and insights consciously.

Q) So, the nous in the heart and head are of the same substance. And so, is the soul?

A) Yes. The soul has a nous. It has cognition and awareness of itself. The nous pours out of the heart when we are awake and we feel our limbs, tendons, and muscles, all our body parts. However, when we are asleep this energy goes back to the heart, and we do not feel anything. In the night, from time to time, we feel an ache or soreness somewhere, but we are not attentive to it. Now, the connection between the nous-energy and prayer of the heart is that the nous-energy, our awareness, goes back to the heart from where it came as we awoke.

Q) But then, are we going back to sleep?

A) Nope! Because the nous returns to the heart gradually, a little at a time. First a man repents, he goes to church, has a pinch at the heart. Then he prays with the prayer book, with the Jesus Prayer and feels compunction. Now he takes only a portion of his nous from the head (at maybe a 50% ratio) and lets it drop down to his chest. All this time he is alert.

Q) You have explained this. Is the ratio so important? You've said it will change.

A) We cannot lose ourselves in prayer. We must be in control with somebody on the watchtower to look out for trouble. We need the brain to recognize the enemy when he is on the offensive. Still, the percentage will fluctuate at times.

Q) What about the saints who were lost in ecstasy?

A) One must have guidance to achieve ecstasy and we are not striving for ecstasy. This is the problem here: in order to achieve noetic prayer, a person needs a guide in order to learn not to succumb to fantasy. However, with guidance a person can pray mystically because this is really how everyone in the past used to pray.

Q) What about those worries of deception?

A) This is almost impossible to occur. If you ever hear of such a thing, know that there are other issues at play. A man cannot be deceived by pronouncing the Jesus Prayer inside himself. Someone who spreads these rumors envies those who do know how to pray this way. We cannot speak in haste concerning something of such grandeur. We listen first, evaluate, search scripture, then we judge or discern. People in this world have prayed with their heart since day one.

Q) Is it that easy to be misled about prayer?

A) Yes, it's that easy. It is innate in us to pray by ourselves in our private room as the Christ tells us in the Gospels. To speak to Him One-on-one. So, it is easy to be misled thinking that we can't pray this way. This, my friends, is the delusion of the age. Prayer of the heart is for all occasions, all times for the great majority of the people. What does a man say when he faces sorrows, "LORD HAVE MERCY"!

Q) Ecstasy is out. How about "Theoria?"

A) Theoria, to see the things of God, to behold Himself as Light, is for the chosen few. We do not know how to curb our gluttony, and we are going to see the "Uncreated Light?" Let's be real.

Q) Are techniques of noetic prayer the same for men and women?

A) This prayer for men is hard. The ladies are talented and easily go into true prayer with tears and supplications, with love and devotion. It is because they feel their heart easily. Prayer starts when one begins to feel his or her heart down there slightly left of center, in the chest area.

Q) How can we help ourselves to feel the heart?

A) To find your heart take easy little breaths and let your focus/nous descend through the neck, straight down into your chest. With a little patience and practice you will begin to feel inside the rib cage. You might even feel the heart pulsating. Explore with the nous all around this inner area - inside your upper torso - as if you are trying to find a way out. Keep searching and you will find the heart, at last.

Q) Could you tell us more about it?

A) The heart is the gateway between this physical world and the spiritual. Our fleshly heart is affected by what occurs in the metaphysical realm. It is agitated or calm, hard or tender, fired up or cool and collected. It acts according to what comes into us through its gates. On the flip side, our spiritual condition can be made better by way of the physical heart. So, by soothing our physical heart to make it peaceful, this can also improve our spiritual condition.

Q) They say take a deep breath and relax. Is this what you mean?

A) Definitely. When you get worked up and the heart is bubbling and ready to burst, calm it down with choppy little inhalations. Slow down the beat and the temptation will most likely dissipate. See that? Here, at this location, where our physical heart is found, the two worlds, spiritual and physical, meet and they interplay in a most inexplicable manner.

Q) What else can you tell us about the heart and the descent of the nous into it?

A) Have you ever seen a snail? The snail lives in a shell. When it discerns that there is no danger, it comes out of its shell. Well, the nous lives in the heart as if in a shell. When we sleep, our nous is contained in its shell, our heart. When we awaken the snail comes up to our head. The nous, as the snail, is something alive, being aware of everything, whether physical or spiritual. When all of its consciousness is up at our head, where we need it in order to solve questions and analyze information, then we cannot pray with feeling and love for the Lord. To pray well, we must make the snail, our nous, lower itself down into its shell, our heart. Then the prayer shifts from being cerebral to being heartfelt. When the prayer is heartfelt it has emotion, a quality we need when praying.

Q) And how again do we lower the snail, our nous, down to its shell?

A) We bring our focus down there. Our nous has the attention we need to pray with all our heart, mind, and strength. So, to fulfill this Great Commandment we make our focus descend into our chest, thus returning the nous to the heart.

Q) We are back to square one. Could you pray for us, Father, that we do this as you have taught us?

A) I will. But you must also help yourself. Be careful of the senses, especially the sense of sight. Do not give the demons weapons to fight you with, for the senses have their roots in the heart which is the seat of desire. The senses are subject to addiction (syndromes, to use modern jargon). Also, fellows, protect your children; this is the information age, they should not be allowed much time to play with the screens and absorb the filth that is displayed on them aplenty.

Q) We thank you. Can I ask something? What do you recommend doing for sleeping disorders?

A) Let me tell you about something that happened recently: a twenty-one-year-old was healed of night terrors. One of our monks told him to put a pocket-size icon of the Mother of God in the chest pocket of his shirt or pajama top before going to bed and to read a part of the Akathist to the Most Holy Theotokos. This youth has not had a terror attack since. It has been a year and a half since the last symptom of a condition which afflicted him persistently his whole life!

Q) You think this will help anyone, with any issue?

A) Look, for whatever it's worth to you, I have told you about the gateway of our heart, about the tremendous influence that the Panagia has on her Son our God, and about the Akathist. If one trusts in the Lord and in the intercessions of His Holy Mother, he or she can do the same prayer to stop any advance of the evil one. I will also tell you; this boy went to this renowned hospital recently to do tests sometime after he started the prayer and sleeping with the icon in the pocket. He only wanted to know if there was any sign of illness or remaining trouble from a plight which had terrorized him for over twenty years, and they found no signs. It has vanished.

Q) Are Her intercessions that powerful?

A) The Theotokos truly saves! Here in our small monastery, she is our guardian, our mother and our joy. She gives the prayer of the heart to those who ask her with humility and with yearning. But then what does the Queen of Heaven not provide? One thing is needed for our prayers to be answered, and that is faith. We must believe.

Q) Hmm. Panagia gives the prayer. But why noetic?

A) All prayers are good, but this one is special. Guys, when you pray, you do not want to think. For instance, when you pray for others, for your family, or for the world just say the Jesus Prayer and let God help them. Do not think of faces, problems, solutions, probabilities, reasons, and do not change the ending of the prayer just say: "Lord Jesus Christ, have mercy on me." The "ME" includes all of humanity.

Q) Is there another reason why we pray noetically?

A) There, in the heart, is the Holy Spirit. St. Isaak the Syrian says that the heart (the cavern in our chest) and the Lord's bridal chamber is one and the same! Draw the nous down below the neck and you will start to feel heaven yourself. My Geronda of blessed memory used to tell us that the heart is a gold mine. If we enter therein, we are likely to get rich.

Q) How far can we take prayer of the heart?

A) Good question. There is a point that we cannot go beyond. I told you about the spiritual world of the angels and demons, a world we cannot enter. It is absolutely forbidden. As for

Theoria, again, it's a no-no, for we need a guide. Without a guide, we would not know if what we see is fake or real, as it is impossible to distinguish between the two. So, we reject everything out of the ordinary. We stay on the well-trodden path. This is the way of the Holy Fathers.

Q) What if we see Christ or a saint?

A) Who am I to see Christ? Listen, the people who see the saints and lights are predisposed to such phenomena before they have occurred. It is the same with dreams, almost. When I go to sleep hungry, what will I see in my sleep? When I love a saint and I am dedicated to his memory I might see the saint; this does not mean that I am really seeing the saint and, even if I were, what good will it do to me? Why take a chance? So, I reject the vision and do not pay attention.

Q) Does the nous have to be in the physical heart?

A) When we say heart, this can mean the greater area, or the place, where the heart is located. When the Fathers say, "put your nous at the heart" they mean "close to the heart." What they are actually saying is AT the heart not IN the heart. Though, if it happens to go in, well, that is fine.

Q) So, the heart can mean the whole lung area?

A) Yes. Some people feel their fleshy heart there somewhere left of center in their chest. Some people feel the outside surface of the chest close to their heart. Yet others do not feel their heart but something like an opening below their neck, like an entrance to a room. They lower their nous into this room in their chest and do not let it move out of there.

Q). As I understand it, during this prayer our consciousness changes?

A) Exactly. The mind rests from the hustle and bustle of its intellectual productivity. The majority of our consciousness shifts down below, and we are not able to go into a labyrinth

237

of complex analytical thought. You know, we avoid the train of brain-busting thoughts that come around to take us for a ride. Not that we do not like it, it's stimulating to think and stuff, but this is to be avoided during prayer.

Q) So, emotions override our thoughts at this time?

A) The heart is about emotion and love, those kinds of things. When you love a person, you do not think about it. This is why, along with the techniques I have shown you, is good to put some zest into our prayer. I remember someone in my family, she has passed away, used to press down at her heart as she breathed out. She would burst into tears from the emotional longing of being with the Lord along with this little push, and that was her method.

Q) Did she push down at the heart using her hand?

A) No, not with hands. She pushed the air down to feel the heart. Try this: Breathe out gently and you will feel your heart settling in its place comfortably. When folks sigh in Church this is a sign that their heart is troubled, with this little push of the air outward the heart is consoled somewhat.

Q) What about the tears? How can we learn to cry?

A) There are some things you can try. One is to think of the many benefactions which come from above, or the Panagia's love for mankind. You can also learn to push down toward the heart for a kick start. Also, to think of something that makes you cry, even if it's worldly. When the tears start to flow you forget the worldly thought and graft these tears onto the tree of prayer.

Q) When I am emotional while praying or afterwards, I get a warmth here in my heart. What is this?

A) This happens often to those who pray well. This warmth enhances their holy effort and can increase the desire for prayer, tenfold. They will know if it is from God. This peaceful feeling derives from love for the Lord and from a repentant heart. Now, there are those who get out of hand and start thinking weird thoughts, such as believing they have accomplished a great feat. What can you say? And yet we have others who, when hearing of something like this happening, disregard any notions about enhancement of prayer or love and repentance. If that's what makes them happy, who am I to disagree?

Q) Why are our emotions frozen solid? We do not even believe in miracles today.

A) Because we live in luxury. We do not need God; we do not need anybody. We have everything: material wealth of a kind no prior generation has ever known is at our disposal. We are spoiled for choices and can always get the best of each kind. In the past, the housewives, the farmers, the maids and servants, the doctors and all peoples wholly depended on the Lord for everything! Do not talk about miracles anymore, they are fairy tales to most people. Now people do not believe, and they do not pray. And if you happen to cry in church, out of love for God, they will think that you have problems at home.

Q) Can I say something? It helps me to be focused before God if I pause with my breath sometimes.

A) When we breathe in "Lord Jesus Christ..." and pause for two seconds, we help the mind refocus because the thinking process undergoes a trial. You see, when the breathing stops, the thoughts stop, and our focus regains a hold on the nous.

Q) Did you say the thoughts stop? I didn't know that.

A) There is a lot you do not know (laughs). This is true, if you try holding your breath for five seconds, you will see that no conceptual images or any thoughts whatsoever have come into view. Another technique to stop thoughts in prayer is to move the eyes about in somewhat rapidly from place to place around the room or area you are in. When the eyes keep moving the faculty of imagination cannot produce the images we need in order to think. When the eyes are still that's when the "movie" of our thoughts and fantasy begins.

Q) What other ways do you have to help us?

A) If you are outside and you want to do a little komboschini (prayer rope), then look far away into the distance at a cloud, or at a point on a treetop. Glue your gaze there and you should be fine. Also, you will not have fantasy if you keep your mind, your nous, outside your peripheral vision.

Q) What can we do if we have images in mind that cannot be easily erased?

A) A renowned monk in the country island of Cyprus had revealed, years back, his way of dealing with unwanted mental impressions. He said the Jesus Prayer and he closed and opened his eyes a few times. I have tried it, and it works; the blinking of the eyes erases fantasy. And as I have told you before, pain and discomfort are enemies of sinful imagery. This is how the monks in the Egyptian deserts dealt with it.

Q) Tell us how monasticism today differs from that of the Egyptian Fathers?

A) The monks then were men of steel. Not like us weaklings. I think that the Holy Fathers in the beginning of the last millennium envisioned these current days of great laxity and carelessness and left us an inheritance of patristic writings to teach and support us. Apart from the self-denial that the early monks practiced, their foundation had always been, as it will continue to be, the Name of Jesus. So, a Christian today can reach a satisfactory level of holiness by exercising the virtues of humility and of patience which takes the place of voluntary suffering.

Q) And also, the virtue of noetic prayer?

A) That's a fact. Noetic prayer is the cornerstone of all endeavors for the sake of the Kingdom of God. What did the Lord say? "The Kingdom of God is within you." The key to this kingdom is God's Name. The demons tremble when they hear "Jesus". They can't stand His Name: it burns them.

Q) Do we say the prayer in our head or in our chest?

A) When we invoke the divine Name mystically, the inner voice is the source somewhere by our heart. Some people feel it being said in their head and that's good, too.

Q) Sometimes I can't feel my heart to put my nous there. What can I do?

A) It takes practice and patience. For some it is easier than for others. So, try this: slightly open your mouth and draw a good amount of air into your lungs with one long breath. Then close your mouth. You have trapped your nous, your focus, inside of you. Without letting your focus escape, breathe out through the nose. When you do this, you will feel your nous settle nicely by the heart. Do this a few times as the lung area expands like a balloon, close your mouth and breathe out through the nose. Soon, you will come to feel the whole area inside your chest.

Q) Father, when I feel my heart, I can perceive its size and shape. Could you comment?

A) This happens naturally. When we concentrate our awareness on a certain body part, we faintly start to see it. Do not let this surprise you. When the holy elders and hermits place the nous inside them, they apprehend and see the location of the heart and its surroundings in depth. They also see the temptations - by the grace of God - which come to entice and capture their attention.

Q) They see the temptations even?

241

A) A temptation most times takes on a form according to the passion it represents, and the nous sees this form by way of its spiritual vision. So, it quickly evaluates it to know what the temptation is selling. This happens in seconds, lightning quick. The experienced monk ignores it completely.

Q) Why aren't laymen able to perceive trouble and to ignore it so quickly?

A) There are several reasons. First of all, they do not have nepsis (watchfulness) nor do they want to make an effort to acquire watchfulness. People today are used to having their way. A quick swipe of the credit card and you have whatever you want. Who needs tears, prayer, attentiveness over the thoughts, and all the gifts of the Spirit? The second reason is unbelief. When believers themselves dismiss the idea that it is possible to acquire prayer today, it becomes self-fulfilling, and it won't be possible for them. Finally, there is negligence, or "acedia", as they call it, which is the biggest temptation.

Q) Can you find other reasons?

A) Yes: excuses. The excuse that there is no time to spend in prayer. The excuse of fear and uncertainty that what I am saying is wrong. And, of course, there is attention deficit. Try to sit in prayer for a few minutes and you will see what I mean. You get the shakes, you suddenly remember you need to look something up on your phone, answer a text, set up an appointment... Try to spend a few quiet minutes in prayer and you will suddenly remember a million other things you need to do right now.

Q) You mention attention deficit and it seems like we all have it. What can we do?

A) Spiritual work. The thoughts that proceed from the heart contain wisdom and foolishness, kindness and cruelty, humility and selfishness, joviality and ill-temperedness and everything in-between. They are all a mix and we, as Christians, are called to sort them out and to arrange the nice thoughts neatly on shelves in our memory, and to delete the rest. To be able to do this we need God close by. He is going to show us how to do this, but we need to be attentive and we need to push ourselves! Matthew says, "the violent take it [the Kingdom of Heaven] by force", and St. John Chrysostom explains "the 'violent' are those who have such earnest desire for Christ that they let nothing stand between themselves and faith in Him." We must fight for prayer and the spiritual life.

Q) Synergy is also needed, correct?

A) Yes. There is an interaction between Him and insignificant man. We need to be attentive of what's going on in a spiritual plane. The mind, being spirit, can penetrate through the clouds of ignorance, but it needs the brain to be aware. God illumines but man consciously accepts. So, I would say, try to find some time to sit, relax and say the Prayer attentively.

Q) Is that all?

A) Believe it or not, that's all needed. If we sit and chill out for a bit, clear our minds and focus by saying the Jesus Prayer, and concentrate on the holy words pronounced, without allowing mental interference, we slowly come to ourselves, our nous gathers and it becomes the recipient of spiritual gifts. One of these gifts is attention - vigilance.

Q) Once again. What is the connection between vigilance and the movement of the nous toward the heart?

A) This is a good question to ask since we are now preparing to come to the end of our talk. There are two kinds of awareness, let us say. One is in the head and the other in the heart. The type of awareness that is in the head is uncertainty, temptations, distraction, worries, and anxiety. When our nous is always "upstairs" the doors of Hades are open, and things are liable to come into our head. So, the shifting of the nous toward the heart plays a role of paramount importance in achieving stillness of thought. The awareness of the heart attracts divine intervention in regard to vigilance.

Q) So, the techniques used to shift focus are very important?

A) These techniques are life! They are not regular tricks per se. When we shift our focus/attention into the lung area, the heart receives the active state of the Prayer, it is sanctified in time. Do not take prayer of the heart lightly and do not assimilate it to other secular or eastern-style practices. St. Gregory Palamas went to great troubles to defend the hesychasts (himself being a prominent member of this group).

Q) What do we expect to find once we start to practice noetic prayer?

A) God. The Kingdom of God is inside of us, and it is in a specific place, here in our heart. We forget this sometimes and we look for God up in the sky. God is closer to us than we think and all we have to do is to reach down with the chief organ of prayer, our nous, inside the cavern of our chest and enclose it within.

Q) We do this by our awareness. Is that right?

A) Yes. The nous, the "eye of our soul" has a noetic sensation, and we can guide this sensation inside of us by physical means. When we feel a certain limb or other body part – pop! – the nous is there instantly. So, we have this liberty to be able to move our nous wherever we put our focus. Therefore, it bears repeating that what we also should expect to find in this prayer is control over our minds and watchfulness. But this comes gradually.

Q) We know that it is late, but please can you tell us something about anxiety?

A) Certain jobs and lifestyles are causes for frequent cases of anxiety, as are unconfessed sins and conflicts with people. A man should ensure that he includes a little physical work in his routine: workout and break a sweat. Adrenaline floods the heart of people who live sedentary lifestyles and sit in front of the screen for hours. Go for a walk, run, play sports, these are good things. Also, always remember to do part of the Akathist to the Theotokos daily. And, of course, noetic prayer also helps immensely. Let's try an exercise: take a deep breath and calm your heart. Have you got it?

Q) This is very calming, isn't it?

A) You can take a deep breath now and then and relax by saying the Prayer to Jesus. Keep your attention away from your head and down towards your heart, and you will not have so much stress. Anxiety and stress are related to unnecessary and harmful intellectual productions, as well as the sinful scenarios of anger, envy, lust, and pride.

Q) Could you please explain it to us one more time? This issue of head and heart?

A) Let me see... the heart is the source of all our thoughts, good and bad, and they manifest along with the evils that I just mentioned up in the "office" (the head). The computer, our brain, will process, analyze and sort them out one by one. Then the nous, being the boss, rejects or accepts these thoughts and may put them into action or just store them in memory. If the nous accepts them, we pay the consequences...

Q) But why do we suffer if we have rejected these ugly thoughts?

A) Excellent. You have asked a good question. I was coming to this. You see fellows, even though we reject an evil offer, still, just by appearing they can shake us up. How many times we are in church, and we see logismoi of the worst kind, and there is nothing we can do. There are also feelings that might appear as premonitions, as sentiments, as instincts, or emotions. Additionally, even rejected thoughts can leave a residue of evil energy that disturbs the heart. Sometimes just an irregular heartbeat is a forerunner of an evil attack to terrorize us...

Q) Please continue, we are all ears!

A) We go through our daily life like a Little Red Riding Hood, trying to act with good intentions but being tricked and manipulated by the evil one. There are places and things with which we come in contact which emit demonic energy that we cannot perceive with our senses. However, our heart perceives it and is affected, and it starts to tremble and flutter.

Q) Father, is this for real? You are talking about me.

A) Why do we bless the house or a car? Why do we cross ourselves? Why do we have icons in our homes? Or why do we make Orthodox friends? To be safe. Do not forget that we are physically immersed in an energy field: the other world. Did we not talk of the other side which is forbidden for us to flirt with?

Q) Didn't you explain this to us?

A) Of course, I did. So, all these thoughts, things, places, ideas, intuitions each carry their own kind of energy generated by demonic or angelic activity. Demons are all over us. Only God can prevent them from entering and sometimes they slip in subconsciously to teach us to be always on guard. We must prepare, we cannot wait for an attack and then have to fight, but we must take precautions beforehand.

Q) Hmm... Do we not all have to start being more cautious?

A) You want to play it safe. What I am saying is this, for one last time: help yourself. To prevent the thoughts from appearing out of the blue, put your guard at the gates. Why do you have mood swings suddenly when you least expect it? Because the thoughts are coming in. So, find some time and let your nous descend down to your heart and pray there. Give the "guys at the office" a break.

Q) Is this movement of the nous that important? Can't we just repeat the prayer by mouth?

A) To say the Jesus Prayer orally is a lifesaver. We start from there. But the result is amplified when we take a few minutes in the morning or evening to pray from the heart. We have a cup of coffee or tea to be alert, and we gather ourselves away from the tumult of modern living. Then we give our inner voice the Jesus Prayer and invoke it slowly, gently, to calm our heart. Thus, we prepare ourselves for battle. Look at us monks. There is no sin here, improper attire, disgraceful behavior, insolent chatter among the guests, heavy perfumes. And yet we are "all eyes": always watchful!.

Q) Can we reach this plateau at some point?

A) Naturally. It will happen sooner or later. You must put in the hours like in flying school and will be amazed how much wiser you will come to be concerning spiritual matters. Down the road you may even help others.

Q) I have a question. Tell us, Father, how do you pray?

A) I will tell you, what did Fr. Cleopa of Romania say? "Patience, patience, patience, patience, patience." I try to have patience during a trial. Then every morning at about 1 AM I have a coffee to be alert. Meanwhile the Jesus Prayer is on my lips. I stand before the Lord to thank him for the day, that I am still alive, that I have my health, my brother monastics, that I have food to eat, clothing and shelter. I also thank him that I am Orthodox. After this I sit to pray with my nous in my heart for about an hour and a half.

Q) With entreaties, requests and such?

A) How do I know that what I ask for will be good for me? No, I do not pray with entreaties. I close all the entrances to my brain, my senses, my heart and I repeat like a beggar in need: have mercy, have mercy, Lord Jesus mercy on me. I do not want replies from God, I just want to love Him. If I hear anything at the time I am praying in my heart, I know it is the evil one. I do not want to hear, see, imagine, think or smell anything at this time. Just "Lord Jesus Christ have mercy on me."

Q) Aren't you in need of anything?

A) No. Just as I feed the barn cats every morning, God feeds me. The Lord tells us not to worry as our Heavenly Father knows our needs but to "seek first the Kingdom of God". Noetic prayer is not like the usual prayers we say at different times. Here we are seeking the Kingdom of God! It is prevention and silence. Why do I need to make requests? Indeed, why do I need to chant hymns and praises to the King of Glory, to His satellites, servants, and His courtiers, and try to get on His good side in order to get this or that? I would rather be like His son, to be able to go into His private quarters. When one prays undistractedly in his heart, he is with the Lord, One-on-one, in the inner chambers of His palace! Now... is that all? Have I answered all your questions?

Q) I have, I think, a last one. Again please, can you lead us through the entrance of the heart?

A) I am going to give you another technique to help. "Heart," as I told you, can also mean the greater area in our chest, like a courtyard around the physical organ of the heart. We go into this courtyard by either pulling our nous in there with the air as we inhale or by pushing it down with our breath as we exhale. We can think of the nous, without imagining it, as a small anchor descending into a fishbowl or a pebble dropping

248

slowly inside of us like in a vessel of water. It also may feel as if the nous is lowered past our neck into a cave below. After we go into this cave, we close all entrances and keep the feeling within, as now there are boundaries that the nous cannot break through to exit.

Q) I have felt this. It is really cozy inside. How can I bring it on spontaneously?

A) It takes practice. Try this all of you: As you look straight ahead create, by feeling, a hollow in your chest; a large empty space. In there is contained your bodily heart which is located slightly left of center. Now, without the use of imagination, place your nous in the middle of this hollow. Do you feel that?

Q) Yes. I do feel it. And now?

A) Let the nous move around along the inside of this enclosure, if it has to, as it unsuccessfully tries to find a way out. Thus, you keep if occupied in there and this will help you to regulate the thoughts coming in and to adjust when you are tempted. Initially, we want our nous on, or around, the heart for defense and to help us to pray undistractedly. With time, noetic prayer comes of age and, if God wants, the spiritual heart's participation may increase to a much greater degree. Then our prayer becomes unceasing.

Q) So, the nous does not have to be inside the physical heart?

A) The Spirit of God is found in the heart, but it is not limited by any perimeter of any sort. You rest your focus anywhere close by and you will make the connection. It is a fact according to my learning and experience that, when the nous returns like this to its source and cuddles against the fleshly heart, or close by, it is renewed spiritually, and the zeal of a man is multiplied.

Q) Let me ask something. I almost see and feel my heart tangibly. Is that ok?

A) To perceive the physical heart by feeling is very good, and then when the feeling intensifies the spiritual eyesight kicks in. But it is not a mirage; still, we should not want this. A man just knows what the body part he is feeling looks like. Let me show you how that works. As an example: Let your arm hang by your side away from your view finder. You will not see it at all. Now, squeeze it into a fist and open your fingers, close them again and, without realizing it, in your mind's eye you see your hand moving. How is this possible? With sense perception. You will perceive only the outline of your hand very faintly but that's enough to draw all your attention there.

Q) So, is this not fantasy?

A) No. But I would not urge you to pursue doing this. Keep your mind clear, I would say. Focus on the words of the Prayer and do not lose control of your thoughts. Let your nous return to the heart in the circular motion described by the Holy Fathers. That is, feel your physical heart, that's all.

Q) It's that simple? And this is the circular motion they talk about in the books?

A) Yes. The wise of this world cannot comprehend the simplicity of it all. St. Theophan puts it this way, "draw down the attention of the nous into the heart and call upon Him there. With the nous firmly established in the heart, abide before the Lord with awe and devotion. If you do this always, then passionate desires would never arise, or any other thoughts." You have to remember to pray with love for God as you do this. You can try something else: feel the nous as a spirit, which it is, and breathe it into your chest. Then push it down so to keep your head empty and try to have it stay down.

Q) Sometimes I am all eyes and I ward off thoughts quickly. Can you comment?

A) When the spirit of the nous is pulled in and we pray with attention and zeal, which means that the nous is safely hidden down below into us, watchfulness is then made easy and before conceptual images can appear, the nous has already acted quickly to have them shuffled away. This is the awesome power of the nous when it unites with the heart. This is called neptic prayer.

Q) Father, when do techniques suffice? Can we pray without them?

A) When we are all fired up, we embrace the Lord and flee away from this vain world. With tears and emotion do we enter another realm. Long words, then, and techniques, bows, prostrations, and petitions are unnecessary. But unfortunately, in our state of mind, it does not last. So, to extend the time spent in graceful communion with God, but even to occupy ourselves with some kind of devotional prayer during dry spells when we feel as if God is absent, we have these techniques to help us along. And they are of extreme importance. You have no idea how precious these techniques and methods are.

Q) Do monks also go through dry spells?

A) More so than the average layman. Our dry spells are like going to hell and back. Therefore, I say to any Orthodox layman, priest, father confessor, novice, monk, priestmonk: Help yourself. Do not settle for the regular morning and evening prayers only. Visit older monks, inquire as to how to do battle against evil. Do not go to a monastery or convent and act like you are at the zoo; go to ask and learn.

Q) Please do continue? We appreciate your input.

A) Our time is running short as we are going to matins soon, but at least you listen, and you ask questions. This, practicing and teaching the art of prayer, is what I like and what I have done throughout my life. But now it is time for you to start putting what we have discussed into action. When I see you next year after Pentecost, I will ask for an account of what you've accomplished. A few final thoughts: you are going to learn by example, and you will learn even more by volunteering at a soup kitchen and putting your faith into action! Please, read the Philokalia, go to fathers who are not afraid to clean a chicken coop, or who toil manually in the fields. They are still around. And do not be afraid of using time-proven techniques and methods tested by real professionals in warfare as the spiritual planes emerge overhead, and the bombs are falling.

Q) You do believe in what you are selling, don't you?

A) I would not be here if I did not believe. I can't fake it. And woe to me if, by my actions and words, I obstruct those who want to achieve their full development in Christ! What? Am I going to tell them not to pray noetically like St. Gregory Palamas himself suggested they do? Didn't Varlaam of Calabria oppose St. Gregory, the dean of the hesychasts? Didn't Varlaam make fun of the monks who used methods? And Palamas put him in his place, for good.

Q) We thank you so much, Father, for your hospitality and kind words. Could you now bless us?

A) God bless you and keep you healthy. If it is His will, we will meet again. Please pray for me also and for our brotherhood. Good night. Have a good day tomorrow and a safe trip. Call on the Lord, my brothers, and His sweet Mother, our Panagia. Today, we need all the help we can get. Let us all unite in prayer.

A HOMILY ON PRAYER

Sermon *"The Jesus Prayer: Artillery Against the Devil"* delivered Dec. 3, 2023, by Fr. Mousa Haddad

In the Name of the Father and of the Son and of the Holy Spirit. Amen.

There's nothing more important in the Christian life than prayer. What oxygen is to the body, prayer is to the soul. It's our lifeline to God. Without prayer, we would spiritually suffocate. St. Ephraim of Katounakia says that all prayers are good and holy, but there's one prayer that's above all prayers, one prayer that's the queen of all prayers, and that one prayer is the Jesus Prayer: "Lord Jesus Christ, have mercy on me." In this morning's gospel, when the blind man begging by the roadside was told that our Lord was passing by, he cried: "Jesus, Son of David, have mercy on me!" This invoking of the name of Jesus is the most powerful tool given to Christians.

We see this emphasis on the name of Jesus from the very beginning of the life of the church... it's nothing new. In chapter 3 of the Book of Acts, when the crippled man at the gate of the temple asked Peter and John for alms, the Apostle Peter said: "Silver and gold I do not have, but what I do have I give you; in the name of Jesus Christ of Nazareth, rise up and walk!" St. Paul, in his Epistle to the Philippians (2:9-10), says that God so highly exalted the Name of our Lord and given Him the Name which is above every name, that at the Name of Jesus every knee should bow, in heaven, on earth, and under the earth.

That's why St Paisios calls the Jesus Prayer "heavy artillery against the devil." The Name of Jesus is invoked

253

because nothing is more powerful. Satan and his demons fear His Name more than anything else. Notice as soon as the blind man in today's gospel begins to cry out saying "Jesus, Son of David, have mercy on me," he's rebuked and told to be silent. Satan does not want anyone to say the Name of Jesus... he does not want us to say the Jesus Prayer.

The holy Apostle Paul in his First Epistle to the Thessalonians (5:17) commands us to pray without ceasing... in other words, to always be in a state of prayer, constantly having the remembrance of God in our heart. And ultimately, this is the purpose of the repetition of the Jesus Prayer... to train us not to forget that we are always in his presence. No matter where you are or what you're doing, the Jesus Prayer is a prayer that can be cultivated in your heart at all times... "Lord Jesus Christ, have mercy on me." It's a short prayer that's easy to remember. St Ephraim the Syrian says: "Whether you are in church, or in your house, or in the country; whether you are guarding sheep, or constructing buildings, or present at drinking parties, do not stop praying."

And this is much easier said than done. Since the fall, man's mind, his nous, has become darkened and is easily distracted. The main purpose of the Jesus Prayer is to gather our attention and to focus on the one thing that's needful, our Lord and Savior Jesus Christ. It doesn't help that we live in an age of constant distractions... distractions that keep us from remembering God, distractions that continually shift our attention away from God and unto earthly cares and material things. Technology has become the source of most of our distractions these days and has harmed our ability to be attentive, especially in our youth.

Even the way social media apps are designed encourages distraction. How often do you see people scrolling through their phone, from one post to another? Giving a few seconds of attention from one idea to another, from one image to another, from one video to another. This is training our mind (our nous) to be so distracted that it's unable to focus on something for a prolonged period. How many kids are being diagnosed with ADD or even ADHD? They can't focus in class or on homework, they can't focus in prayer or at church, they can't focus when they're being spoken to or given instructions. Technology, whether it's phones, tablets, video games, TV, has shortened their attention spans. And what do we do when we want our children to calm down or we just need a break from them? We give them phones, tablets and let them play video games or watch TV for hours on end. It's an addiction that we keep feeding. These games and apps are designed to make you addicted.

And there are some things you can do to end this vicious cycle... limiting access to technology, setting timers, restricting social media usage. But the most beneficial thing you can do for your child is to give them a prayer rope and teach them the Jesus Prayer. The prayer rope is designed to help us gather and focus our attention in one place to keep us from being distracted. While using the prayer rope we focus all of our attention on the knots as we touch them one by one, saying at each knot: "Lord Jesus Christ, have mercy on me." Eventually, the goal is to transfer that attention from the prayer rope to the physical heart, but that's for another sermon.

How can we teach our children the Jesus Prayer, if it's not a part of our own life. How can we give them this precious gift of the Jesus Prayer if we don't have it? I'd like to challenge each and every one of you to begin practicing the Jesus Prayer. If you don't have a prayer rope, stop by the bookstore after liturgy. I want to offer you some beginner's advice on how to do the Jesus Prayer. Although the Jesus Prayer should be done all day, it's important that you have undistracted dedicated time in the morning to say the Jesus Prayer in your prayer corner. When we first wake up in the morning, after having rested, there's a certain clarity of mind that we have. The mind is less distracted. It's in a state that allows us to focus better and to draw closer to Christ in prayer.

When you say the Jesus Prayer, say it from the depth of your heart, with fervor and longing, as if you're in the Sahara Desert alone with God... as if you're a mother or father begging for food to feed your starving children... "Lord Jesus Christ, have mercy on me." If you feel distracted as you're doing the Jesus Prayer, distracted with a multitude of thoughts, say the prayer out loud, with your prayer rope in hand. St Ephraim of Katounakia says: "Say the prayer... Say each word one-by-one with attention, with understanding. Do not proceed to the second word if you have not comprehended the first. Emphasize the ending more, that is, 'have mercy on me.'" "Lord Jesus Christ, have mercy on me."

As we say the prayer, the Holy Fathers teach that we must be deaf, mute and blind. In other words, completely undistracted. We are not to imagine anything, not to have any image in our mind, not even of Christ or the Theotokos or any of the saints. In fact, they tell us if we have any type of vision as we pray, we must ignore it right away and make the sign of the cross, even if it's a vision of Christ Himself. Oftentimes I hear from people that they have dreams of Christ or the Theotokos or the saints, and they try to decipher what it means. The Fathers say don't give any attention to visions and dreams, ignore them because most of them are not from God.

If the vision or dream is persistent and repeats itself numerous times, you come to the priest for guidance.

As we do the Jesus Prayer, not only are we not to form any images in our mind, but, we are also not to have any thoughts, good or bad. Think about it… what are some of the thoughts you may have during your prayers? "What's on my schedule today?", "do I have to pick up the children?", "do I have to finish any homework?", "what am I cooking?", "what's my agenda at work today?", "did I turn off the lights last night in the basement?" We may think that some of these thoughts are good thoughts, but when we pray, there's no such thing as a good thought. All thoughts, good or bad, when they come during prayer, are from the devil. They are his thoughts. He is so cunning that he makes us believe that they are our thoughts. Don't let what you have to do during the day occupy your mind during prayer. Also, don't let him rush you through your prayers. That's also a temptation he sends our way. "I have things to do, I have to get through my prayers really quick, I'm so busy today." Those, again, are his thoughts, not yours. Our mind can become the playground of demons through imagination… we must not allow it. Dismiss every single thought that comes as coming from Satan himself. The fathers tell us that the devil hates nothing more than the Jesus Prayer so he'll do whatever he can to distract us. St. Paisios Velichkovsky says about the Jesus Prayer that "no other spiritual weapon can so effectively restrain the demons. It burns them as fire burns a wick."

The importance of the Jesus Prayer is not necessarily the quantity of time you spend doing it, but rather, the quality that you give to that time. In other words, don't go home and decide tomorrow morning I'm going to do the Jesus prayer for an hour. You don't want to start so aggressively, and realize how difficult it is, and then stop. Start with minutes every morning and see how that goes. Then you come to your spiritual father and with him discuss how you're doing and how you can develop the Jesus Prayer more so that it can be grace-filled.

Those few minutes you dedicate in the morning to the Jesus Prayer will be the guiding principle of your entire day and fill you with joy. It will inform the way you feel, think, speak and act. The one who does the Jesus Prayer in the morning is like the man who builds his house on a rock. He has laid a solid foundation for the entire day. And eventually, this will lead to a transformation, not only of the day, but of your entire life. You will be transfigured from glory to glory through the practice of the Jesus Prayer.

The more you say the prayer, the more it becomes a part of you. You begin by saying it out loud, then saying it with your inner voice, and eventually, saying it in your heart. This is what the Fathers mean when they say we must "descend with the mind into the heart." You might be wondering, "what in the world does that mean?" It's like when you get a song stuck in your head, you just keep saying it without realizing it. You wake up in the morning and you're singing it, and you can't seem to get it out of your head. That's what we want the Jesus Prayer to become like. You could be sleeping, you could be eating, you could be talking to someone, and the prayer is being said in your heart. That's what St Paul means when he says pray without ceasing.

I would like to end with a quote from St Paisios Velichkovsky. He says: "The Jesus Prayer is work common to angels and humans. With this Prayer people attain to the life of the angels in a short time. The Prayer is the source of all good works and virtues and drives the dark passions far away from man. In a short time, it makes a man capable of acquiring the grace of the Holy Spirit. Acquire it, and before you die you will have acquired an angelic soul. The Prayer is divine rejoicing."

In the Name of the Father and of the Son and of the Holy Spirit. Amen.

EPILOGUE – IMAGINATION AND SPIRITUAL WARFARE

All people use their imagination as they think and, therefore, the devil fights them through fantasy. This is how one falls. No sin occurs if an evil thought does not proceed it by a mental image. To resist, the memory must be empty, for the evil one uses the filth, which modern man accumulates daily, to entice him. This is the information age, but this information comes up unexpectedly at home, at work, or in church, without control.

But now, there is a way to get well and this will happen by way of noetic prayer, which will regulate the thinking process and will bring the mind to Hesychia (stillness).

Thoughts come up from out of the heart so in order to keep the muddiness of thoughts from ascending to the head, the nous (the focus) is brought down to chest level and the prayer is said there. This simple movement of the focus/attention stops the imagination without which thoughts cannot be manifested. This is easy and simple, yet hard to grasp for those who expect something complex and out of the ordinary.

What we are trying to do is to stop imagining and, thus, to alleviate distractions. God will take it from there. Man's soul has the ability to pray well once stillness of thought is realized. Also, when the nous enters the haven of the chest, emotion is achieved. Emotion is a necessary ingredient for pure prayer. To enhance the whole effort needed to pray well, it helps to go to confession regularly and, initially, to keep the eyes open while praying.

Finally, for those who want to excel in prayer, it is imperative to respect, love, and obey the holy priest in their church so that, through his prayers, they may advance in virtue and grow in their faith.

- *A.H.*

INDEX

262

263

www.ingramcontent.com/pod-product-compliance
Lightning Source LLC
Chambersburg PA
CBHW071631140626
46555CB00022B/2055